Tell Me More

Center Point
Large Print

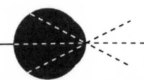

**This Large Print Book carries the
Seal of Approval of N.A.V.H.**

Tell Me More

*Stories About the
12 Hardest Things
I'm Learning To Say*

KELLY CORRIGAN

CENTER POINT LARGE PRINT
THORNDIKE, MAINE

This Center Point Large Print edition
is published in the year 2018 by arrangement with
Ballantine Books, an imprint of Random House,
a division of Random House LLC.

Tell Me More is a work of nonfiction. Nonetheless, some
of the names and personal characteristics of the individuals
involved have been changed in order to disguise their
identities. Any resulting resemblance to persons living or
dead is entirely coincidental and unintentional.

The text of this Large Print edition is unabridged.
In other aspects, this book may vary
from the original edition.
Printed in the United States of America
on permanent paper.
Set in 16-point Times New Roman type.

ISBN: 978-1-68324-709-8

Library of Congress Cataloging-in-Publication Data

The Library of Congress has cataloged record
under LCCN: 2017057504

A lot has happened since the last time
I had a book to dedicate.

I've been to two funerals:
my father's, which was kind of fantastic,
and my friend Liz's, which was devastating.
I left those services,
as most people probably did,
urgently wanting to deserve my life
and the people in it.

This book is about things we say
to people we love
(including ourselves)
that make things better.

It is for Liz, who I think would
have appreciated the effort.
I wish we could have
done this together, Lizzard,
though in a way, we sort of did.

Contents

It's Like This

There was no real reason for it to fall apart that morning. And, in fact, *it* didn't. I did.

I could say it was because my dad—whom I adored to the point of absurdity—had died sixty-eight days before. I could say that watching him shrink into silence did me in, that grief bled me dry, that I was no longer a match for ordinary family life, that my radio station had lost the signal, the drone of static broken only by the occasional reception of two clear thoughts: *He's gone* and *Please give him back*.

But the truth is that I'm always teetering between a mature acceptance of life's immutables and a childish railing against the very same. In the time it takes to get the mail, I can slide from sanguine and full of purpose to pissed off and fuming. As for perspective, there's a Hertz customer service rep in Des Moines who could release a tape of my recent "feedback" that would make the Internet break. All of which is not to say that I can't spot the difference between trivial and tragic. I can. I do. I genuflect in gratitude for my health, my husband, my kids, my central heating. I just can't stay bowed down. I keep popping back up, saying things like, *Does anyone else's back hurt?* In those moments, I'm not that much closer to maintaining an adult frame of reference than I was the day I got my first period.

Speaking of menstruation, lack of perspective, and fits of irrationality, I have two teenage daughters. Georgia is sixteen, with Vidal Sassoon hair, almond-brown eyes, flat feet, and one killer dimple. She likes lacrosse and Snapchat and prefers precalculus and chemistry to the humanities, where there are too many possible answers. Her interest in me hinges on allowance and rides; offering more, like an opinion, visibly chafes her. Her independence tortures and impresses me. She is a world-class procrastinator who brushes her wet hair in the car on the way to the party and waits until we pull up to practice to put on her cleats. She is cool on a dance floor and sometimes, when she's telling me a story, I am as captivated by her as I have ever been by another human being.

Claire is fourteen, has blond hair that turns brown in the winter, size 12 shoes, dark blue eyes she gets from her father, and a smile that can be seen from space. She plays volleyball and basketball because we make her, lacrosse because she likes being outside in the spring. Without our interference, her extracurricular hours would be dedicated to the lyrics of Lin-Manuel Miranda, decorating baked goods with special nozzles she found on Amazon, and throwing theme parties, six a year, pegged to the holidays. She designs her own invitations, finds snack and décor ideas on BuzzFeed, and plugs in a $14 disco light to energize the dance floor that is our deck. In fifth grade, she got every single answer right on a standardized test that was given over four days, but that doesn't mean she can spell "skedule" or "arguement." We like to think she might be some sort of creative genius, but anything is possible.

When they're together, the girls are either watching reruns of *The Office*, ignoring each other in favor of whatever's on their cellphones, or squabbling over how to say Wingardium Leviosa. Sometimes, the way they go back and forth reminds me of the way Edward and I bicker, and I feel sure that if only we had modeled bipartisanship, our children would be better and happier. Once or twice a year, they do a Bollywood routine they learned from Just Dance and I'm reminded of the days when being at home with each other was enough. When they do the Garth & Kat skit from *Saturday Night Live*, I dare to believe I can see the faint edges of a future friendship.

That leaves Edward, my husband. Growing up, he was told he looked like Robby Benson of *Ice Castles*. Now he gets Ben Stiller. His obsessions are swimming, having the proper gear for any occasion, ensuring that each person he comes in contact with has seen and fully appreciated all five seasons of *The Wire*, and the Golden

State Warriors. He fanboys their impetuous power forward, Draymond Green, whom he calls Sack Tapper after Green kicked several players in the nuts during the 2016 playoffs. Other than taking upward of ten days to unpack a suitcase and nagging me about going to the dentist, Edward is fairly easy to live with. He is not afraid of the grocery store or the stove and helps me color the very back of my hair, painting my gray roots Medium Brown 5 with the mini plastic brush that comes with the kit. He is deeply rational, has work that matters to him, and almost always holds my hand as we fall asleep even though he doesn't really like holding hands.

Me, I'm all over the place. I look like my dad, and like both the girls in different ways. My hair is naturally curly but not in the sexy beachy way. If I were a dog, I'd be the kind that's easier to shave down than to groom. I have been told I have large teeth. I'm soft, and getting softer, and my ass is less pumpkin than helipad. To pretend I care enough to fix these things, I exercise every Saturday morning with Edward. I slow down when my forehead starts to shine—I'm not a huge fan of showers. I wear the same clothes all week and often get past noon before putting on a bra or looking in the mirror. I prefer projects to jobs. I've built "furniture," been a "photographer," and started a "company." I am riddled with ideas, a dozen a day. My ambition waxes when I drink alcohol—one skinny margarita can have me filing to run for state senate—and wanes in the morning after the kids leave and I am alone with the work. The one absolutely good thing I do is volunteer for our local children's hospital. Every Tuesday, from three p.m. to five p.m., I hold babies in the NICU.

That's me, that's us.

So, this one morning . . .

I'd slept okay. The usual five a.m. stumble to the loo, and back to the sack for another couple hours in bed until, like curtains snapping open, I am awake. There's bacon cooking—I can smell it—which puts Edward in the kitchen attending to his clockwork need for breakfast meats. I sit up, set my glasses on my nose to read the slight curve of my slippers. Left on left. Right on right. Another day begins.

After I quiet my white-noise machine, the first sound I hear is a bit of edgy back-and-forth between the girls. Someone is wearing someone else's shirt. Without asking. Bickering bothers me much more than it bothers Edward. Edward can tolerate it all day, coming and going, while I launch into action at the first whiff. If smoke always leads to fire, the reasonable mind begs to know, why not douse the kindling *before* the place burns to the ground?

Here's why: Edward read a parenting book

(just one) and the book said "Let 'em fight!"

As for the shirt, a $9 Circo crewneck from Target, it was purchased for Georgia. But last week, when I noticed it in her dresser, overflowing with options she hasn't considered since she committed full-time to black leggings and a gray hoodie, I thought, *Gee, I bet I could get Claire to wear this.* I didn't think Claire would *like* it. I thought I could *get her* to wear it, so it wouldn't go unused. I need things to be used—the heel of the bread, the last page of the notebook, the rug from college. Our car has 148,412 miles on it.

So yeah, I gave Georgia's shirt to Claire. I did not ask permission.

While the shirt thing is going down in the hall, my daughters' voices rising, the phone rings, which suggests, as it does in households across the world, that someone should answer it. But here at Crest Road, the ringing is a dog whistle and I'm the only canine.

"Edward! The phone!"

He can't hear me, what with the crackling bacon, the exhaust fan it necessitates, and the squabble in the hallway.

I hustle to grab the upstairs phone, only to hear "Hi! This is Joan from the Breast Cancer Awareness Fund, calling to talk to you about our Fun Run and Handbag Swap." Oh no, Recording "Joan." No, you don't. I've had breast cancer.

14

Chemo, surgery, radiation, the whole Party Pak. I *gave*. Click.

Meanwhile, the girls are really getting into it. It's more than a shirt now; it's *I always!* and *You never!* and *That's crazy!* Then, Claire goes Real Housewives: "You don't even know how to share, you selfish bitch!"

I am standing over her in seconds. "What did you just say?" Fuck Edward's book.

"She—" Claire starts to answer my rhetorical question.

"Did you hear—" Georgia says.

"Stop! The next person who says one word—" What cherished activity can I afford to kill? Or should I flip it, make the offender *do* something vs. *lose* something? "—will walk Hershey every goddamn day until Christmas!" Taking the Lord's name in vain while invoking his son's birth is a twisted bit of sacrilege, but I've never been the Catholic my parents tried so goddamn hard to raise. "You hear me?"

The girls don't walk the dog because the girls don't care about the dog. We got her because Ms. Judy, a beloved elementary school teacher, leaned in to my ear at Back to School night and said, "Before they hit puberty, get a dog." She swore it was the only thing she'd ever seen soothe the girls once their pituitary glands start whispering to their ovaries. *Of course,* I thought, *a dog.* A thing to love and be loved by. A reliable friend.

15

They did, in the enchanted early days, like the first twenty minutes of Christmas morning, before anyone realizes she got half of what she asked for, but those quickly ended and were followed by a lot of finger-pointing over who has to feed her, followed by contract negotiations with the weaker parent over payment for cleaning up after her. It was soon clear that if Hershey defected to a more devoted family—say Ms. Judy's—not a tear would fall. Put another way, the dog is certainly not as irreplaceable to them as an inanimate bit of cotton available in seventeen colors in a superstore three miles from their home.

"Ladies, someone better call the food photographer!" Edward says. "I've got an award-winning plate of bacon down here!"

They stare at me. We all kind of hate each other in this minute, me most of all because I taught them the word *bitch* and I yell so they yell and Edward missed another brawl so they'll like him more today and he's better anyway and whatever lust for combat my daughters have comes straight from me and I thought I was going to be a good mom like Michelle Constable or Tammy Stedman and I'm not and according to a parenting blog I saw, yelling is as bad as corporal punishment and particularly destructive to self-esteem so oh my God, what am I doing? Soft but direct, I say, "Georgia, Claire is wearing the shirt. I gave it to her. If you want it back, you can have it after today. Now, go."

Georgia turns in a theatrical huff, Claire clomps behind, no less preposterous, and in seconds, I hear my elder tattling on me to her father: "She *always* takes Claire's side."

I took the side of ex-ped-i-ence! I want to scream, but I can't defend myself against my accuser, not only because that would make my daughter equal to me in a way that's verboten according to the last conversation I had with my mother, but also because the phone rings again and it's her, my mom, calling as if she knew I was headed for a doomed arbitration. Just as well. The girls are eating bacon with SuperEdward. What do they care about a T-shirt now?

My mom is some number of years over seventy (she doesn't care for specifics on this point). She loves playing games, everything from gin rummy to those elaborate bracket pools for the NCAA Basketball Tournament. She's quick to suggest a small wager and always pays. She once bet my friend Jamie a buck on a college football game and when she lost, she sent him a fresh one-dollar bill in the mail. She's a mostly retired real estate agent and former blonde who dresses entirely for comfort. She stands about five feet three these days. She raised my two older brothers and me in Villanova, on Wooded Lane, in a house she and my father bought the year her second-favorite movie came out: *The Graduate* (edged out decades later by *Pretty Woman*). Forty-nine years after they moved in, she's calling from that same kitchen, this time for help figuring out how to transfer frequent-flier miles to her account from my dad's. My dad, whose pajamas I'm wearing, had a whopping 3,300 miles on American, enough for a free on-board chicken Caesar wrap. My mom heard from a friend that miles transfer after death. She wants to give me his account number to see if I can figure it out.

I want to help her so much. Just not this way.

Like my mother, I resent small print, forget every password, and fear all forms. In fact, at this very moment, I'm sitting on an expired driver's license rather than face the lines at the DMV even though Edward keeps telling me I can schedule an appointment online, *like that's reliable.* As for my mom, I'd much rather "help" by actually talking about my father, whom we called Greenie, a nickname he picked up in college for reasons involving a bad hangover. I want her to tell me how monochromatic every day seems now that he's gone, how limited the potential of any outing has become, how dull it is to watch the Phillies, go to noon mass, have a Smirnoff on the rocks alone. I want to hear how hollow it feels to live without him after fifty years. Who does she play cards with? But Mary Corrigan does not do this

18

sort of relating. It's not what she needs, not now, not ever. She needs privacy, church, and time—and right this minute, she needs to talk about closing bank accounts, returning his leased Buick before they charge her for another month, and those frequent-flier miles.

While she reads out an account number that I pretend to write down, I imagine Greenie jumping on the line to ask about the "Georgia Peach" and "Claire, Claire, the Honey Bear." The way he said their names you'd have thought they were champion boxers, or halftime performers at the Super Bowl. I notice our neighbor's SUV idling out front, waiting to take the girls to school.

"Where's my backpack?" one of his "super-stars" bellows up the stairs to me in a way that sounds like accusation.

"I don't know. Where did you look?" Edward says, as we were taught to do by the girls' Montessori teachers back in preschool.

"Mom! Where's my backpack?"

I put my hand over the phone. "Where did you look?"

"I put it by the front door."

I take the bait. "Ma—" I can taste the metal hook, the feathery lure in my mouth. "I gotta call you back." Before I'm even halfway down the stairs, I see the shoulder strap peeking out behind the coat closet door. "Oh, come on! It's right there."

"Ugh." She opens the front door, letting in a plane of morning sun that lights up her scalp. Mother of Christ Almighty, is that a nit?

Before I can check, both girls are gone and the door crashes into its frame, popping the knocker up and down, up and down, like the caustic closing beats of a Black Sabbath song. It will be hours before they return and we start again, another opportunity to be functional together, another possible breakdown, another afternoon combing for lice.

Across the kitchen, Hershey whimpers near a pile of eggshells emptying the last of their slime onto the counter. The bacon grease is turning white in the pan. I have not looked in the mirror, or eaten, and there's Edward by the door, showered, shaved and serene, his hand on the knob.

"You going?" I ask.

"To work? Yeah, I'm going to work."

"Good for you." In about four seconds, it will be me alone in this house that has just been sprayed with tension.

"O-kay," he says.

As he opens the door, the air of deliverance upon his cheek, I say, "You see those hair balls? That's what I'm going to do when you leave. Well, first, I'm going to toss your eggshells; then I'm going to get down on all fours and wipe up dog hair from around the table legs—with my hands."

"We should get a Dustbuster."

Yeah, that's the problem. We need a Dustbuster.

The dog barks. "Hershey!" Edward and I say in unison. She barks again. Edward looks at his watch. "You want me to feed her?" he says.

"I got it." I hate myself for being *that wife,* the fed-up, put-out sourpuss that Easy Ed has to make himself keep coming home to. *Snap out of it already,* I think.

"I'll call you after my meeting. We'll figure it out, Kelly," he says, referring, I think, to everything.

"Mm-mm," I say, setting him free, watching him leave, not believing him, this man who agreed to pay his children to clean up after their own dog.

I feed Hershey. My head hurts. It often does in the morning, because at the end of the day, I like to have one strong drink—tequila with lime, or whiskey with bitters—with Edward even though it ruins my sleep and sometimes the next morning too. I take three Advil and drop into the faded linen chair I used to like but has now become the chair where I sit when I have nothing left, my staring chair, my giving-up chair, my grieving chair. I've been sitting here a lot since Greenie died, turning to Hershey for comfort like Ms. Judy promised the girls would, watching Carpool Karaokes, making lists of things I'm pretty sure I won't do. My lips pinch and my chest tightens. I feel tears coming. I let them, because who cares? No one is here to be unnerved or turned off by weakness.

I'm so tired, I could almost fall asleep. I want to call someone, but what is there to say? Looking toward the phone, thinking I might call my cousin Kathy, who is ten years older and knows everything about grief and its pushy, erratic ways, I see a pile of cut fingernails. Or are they toenails?

Scumbags.

"Kelly, my God, they are *children!*" my better self says. Why can't I look at the girls the way Greenie did? Would it be so hard to help my mom with the frequent-flier miles? What if Liz—my dear Liz, who died at forty-six, whom I eulogized not three months ago—can see me storming around my life, bug-eyed over the most predictable misdemeanors, without an ounce of appreciation for our general well-being?

Before I launch into a full offensive against myself, the doorbell rings. A toned and shiny UPS man hands me a large envelope from J.Crew. During a recent bout of procrastination, I'd agonized for twenty minutes over an online purchase. It was just a shirt, but thanks to a month-long affair with Cap'n Carbohydrate, I'm straddling sizes, and when you're trolling the Final Sale section, stakes are high.

I run a knife along the top of the envelope

and lift out a sleeveless linen shell with a jaunty decorative placket, just out of season. The color, a casual, faded red, is even better than it looked online. *This baby's a winner,* I say to myself. Dangling from the armpit is a tag with the unambiguous message "This item cannot be exchanged or returned." Who would want to?

I take the stairs two at a time, drop Greenie's pajama top on the floor in front of my dresser, and shake the *old jessies* (my mother's term) into a minimizing underwire. As I hand-iron the folds of the top, the cut doesn't look as wide as I'd like, but then, wait, it's on me. The placket looks good, the hem's hitting me right at the hip, but across the middle, I am being hugged, hard. Looking over my shoulder in the mirror, I can see the full outline of my bra, including the three rows of hook-and-eye clasps. I reach around to pull it off by the collar, but my C+ cups are holding strong. I try skootching the shell up slowly. Not happening.

Many more minutes of sweaty contortions and obscenities get me nowhere. It seems I will wear this shirt, under everything, forever. Like a corset.

There is only one way out.

Grabbing a pair of the girls' craft scissors to use as the Jaws of Life, I slice open the shirt like an EMT. I'm so mad at J.Crew, and those children, and that husband, not to mention the red-faced madwoman in the mirror that I actually growl, stopping only when I see two women, neighbors, power walking below my window, with their beautiful well-behaved dogs.

I ball up the destruction along with its plastic packaging and stuff it deep in our trash can so I never have to see it again. I pull one of Edward's T-shirts over my head. It's roomy and smells like him, a mix of Mennen Speed Stick and pomade and his own particular odor that I have become accustomed to. At my feet is Greenie's pajama top, the plaid flannel button-down he died in. I bring it to my nose and the day is inside me, the tart cranberry juice untouched on his tray, the stale breath of a man who couldn't eat, the mint of the balm I kept putting on his lips, and a comedic trace of Polident. It makes him seem alive, like me and Edward and Hershey, and then he dies again, right in that moment, and I drop my head.

Without really choosing, I am back in bed. Hershey backs up a few steps and then leaps in beside me. My toes are cold. I dig my fingers into the soft hair of Hershey's jowls and stare at the wall in front of me. There's a cobweb and a line on the baseboard where the vacuum hits the wall. I don't clean enough. Does it matter? Am I letting people down? Where are those Clorox wipes? Maybe I need an office job. A boss telling me what to do. I would hate it so much, but at least I would know where to be and what time to get there.

I have to go to the bathroom, which brings me to the magnifying mirror. I'm fifty and I haven't found any way around looking it. Age spots have surfaced, new ones every month it seems, including one on the tip of my nose that is *thisclose* to being something people will have to work hard not to stare at. When I smile, I have wrinkles *in my cheeks*. Coffee, a nonnegotiable, is making my teeth smoker brown.

Before I sit on the toilet to pee, I load up my electric toothbrush with Sensodyne ProNamel and start the two-minute clean. The old-people toothpaste stings my gums as it fills the gaps a condescending dentist warned me about years ago. *Oh dammit,* I think, rolling my eyes. Claire has an orthodontist appointment this afternoon. I'll have to pick her up early. How come Edward never has to take anyone to Dr. Kasrovi's? And why so many appointments anyway? Can't they combine a few?

Why am I so mad at everyone?

Bubbling up from some well of memory comes "It's *like* this."

That's what Will liked to say, Will the meditation guy from Edward's office, Will who had interesting answers to hard questions and didn't wear shoes. It's been a year since I've seen him and I'm still not totally sure what he meant by *It's like this* but I've come to think of it as

25

This is the way it is, up and down, good and bad, so don't worry, because it's like this for everyone and it's supposed *to be.*

I met Will back when I used to write in a sunny corner of Edward's office—a wonderland of adjustable desks and nap pods, unlimited kombucha and burrito bars. When Edward's boss generously offered me an empty desk and welcomed me to partake in all the employee benefits, including mindfulness sessions with Will, I said, *Amen, brother.*

Will was about my height, with clear eyes and good posture. His conversational pace and all-around composure made him a person I could only communicate with on the days when my marbles aligned. Most of the time, I slipped into his class, lowered myself onto a gray foam brick, and did a crappy version of whatever he told us to do (breathe, notice, release) until he rang the bell from Tibet that meant it was time to open our eyes and return to our regularly scheduled lives. Sometimes, depending on how the class filed out, I'd linger and we'd talk.

One morning, after Will had led us through a meditation about relationships and conflict, I said to him, "When the shit hits the fan in our house, I get kind of crazy—like *furious*-crazy." He did not cringe, so I continued. "In the moment, even when I saw trouble coming from a mile away, I actually feel *shocked*."

He nodded. "It's a very cool feature of the human mind that we keep hoping that our interactions are going to be different."

Come again, Chief Stocking Feet? "Repeatedly expecting things to be better than *you know from experience* they will be—that's cool?"

"I think so. Even if it creates some suffering. Which of course it does." I looked at him funny, but he skated past my scrutiny. "We'd really be in trouble if we gave up on change, on the potential for growth."

"Right, so when I go crazy on people, say my children, I'm just encouraging personal growth."

"Ooh. I see." He'd pinpointed my pathology already. "You have the illusion that you can change people's behavior."

Yup.

"Edward says I have 'vigilante tendencies.'"

Will smiled his meditation-teacher smile. He liked Edward.

"But I want to grow out of the shock. Teenagers are mean and moody. This is not new news. Husbands are late and busy and distracted. Whoopie. You hit a parked car, missed a deadline, lost your phone charger. Oh well, oh well, oh well."

"Oh well." He considered. "I like that. That's good."

"Yeah, me too. Unfortunately, *Oh, well* usually comes out of my mouth as *Motherfucker.*"

He laughed and then, seeing I was not kidding, said, "Accepting things *as they are* is difficult. A lot of people go to war with reality." What Will didn't point out, because he wanted me to arrive there on my own, was that his brand of acceptance wasn't grim compromise or gritted-teeth tolerance. He was not suggesting that we roll over, but rather that we keep rolling, onward.

I already knew this. *Resistance is the road to bleeding ulcers,* I'd joked with Edward. *Resistance is suffering on permanent repeat,* I'd said offhandedly at parties. *Only a fool berates the gods over stretch marks and bad weather and in-laws,* I'd speechified to my girlfriends over cocktails. That was half the reason I bored myself so: I knew better.

"Being in our lives *as they are* is probably one of the most common struggles people have," Will said. "Going back thousands of years."

Oh, my God, I'm a cliché, I thought, wondering if Mr. Don't Go to War with Reality got tired of telling us janky mortals the same thing over and over.

Here I thought I was a special person with Special People Problems that would take a long time to diagnose and maybe even require new forms of treatment, or at least a bit of original advice. But I was everybody; a pocket truism that's been circulating for *thousands of years* would suffice.

I'm done peeing. I flush and tie Greenie's giant pajama bottoms back around my waist. I spit a mouthful of toothpaste into the sink, rinse, and bare my teeth for inspection. I relax my face. I exhale. I console my reflection: *It's like this, Kelly. This is how it goes.*

Hidden in the morning's frustrations, like a rattlesnake in the woodpile, is something else. I close my eyes so I can listen for the other thing—the further-away, much worse thing—in the quiet of my own head.

Life ends. I've known this since the summer of 1972, when an ambulance drove away in silence with the old lady who gave out Almond Joys on Halloween. But now I've seen mortality do its awful ghosting up close—twice—and that has changed the context of everything. In the new zodiac, without Greenie, without Liz, all terms have been recalibrated. Pain is agony. Bad is fatal. The scale is reset, making it hard for me to reconcile what I've seen with how I live.

Liz would have done a week of aggressive bromodomain inhibitors at Cedars-Sinai for one morning of hairballs, eggshells, and toenail clippings. To see her kids become teenagers screaming obscenities at each other in the hall? She'd have given up every organ in her pelvic cavity.

Then there's Greenie, who would have told you that life was a carnival: all music and snack stalls,

29

fortune-tellers and strong men—*It's magical, Lovey!* Edward called Greenie a happiness genius, but ask anyone: he was as excited about being alive as anyone you will ever meet. This isn't just a kid making a hero out of her dad. And me? I walked next to him in that festival light for almost fifty years and then, one night in February, his hand went still in mine and here I am, same as ever, except quicker to anger and thirteen pounds heavier.

Shouldn't loss change a person, for the better, forever?

Maybe Will's curious phrase—*It's like this*—applies here, too. This forgetting, this slide into smallness, this irritability and shame, this disorienting grief: *It's like this*. Minds don't rest; they reel and wander and fixate and roll back and reconsider because it's like this, having a mind. Hearts don't idle; they swell and constrict and break and forgive and behold because it's like this, having a heart. Lives don't last; they thrill and confound and circle and overflow and disappear because it's like this, having a life.

Tell Me More

I had a facial recently. It's not something I usually do, but a nice woman I'd done a favor for gave me a gift certificate to a high-end, full-service spa in San Francisco. I've always felt that facials, which usually include a few invigorating minutes of head and neck massage at the end, are the best value—and I feel strongly about value.

It took forty-five minutes to get across the Bay Bridge and another five to parallel park on a hill that would test my emergency brake. Still, I arrived in the lobby on time. An android-beautiful millennial who seemed particularly well rested welcomed me. The air vibrated with the sounds of flute and harp. A scented candle—let's say jasmine—flickered on the counter. The receptionist asked my name and, after glancing at a quaint paper appointment book, lit up.

"You're with Tish today," she said. "Have you worked with Tish before?"

"First time."

"How *brilliant*."

I changed into a soft robe and stretched out on a well-dressed massage table. The door opened.

"Kelly," Tish said decisively, like she had waited many long years to see me.

"Hi," I said.

Tish was a large blue-eyed woman with a pillowy chest, her hair pulled back in an impeccable bun. Her face was pink, as if she'd just completed an aggressive peel. Once Tish confirmed that I was comfortable, she began doing what estheticians do, her fingers taking a gentle overview of the landscape that was my face.

I felt relaxed, encouraged, I suppose, by the chirps of kookaburras layered over sitar playing. The name Ravi Shankar came to me, followed by the name Bruce MacDonald, a college friend and rabid Ravi fan. I felt a surge of hope; Tish and her healer hands were going to change my face—possibly my life. Then I remembered that nothing short of a surgical instrument changes your face. If exotic oils and gels made any difference, everyone who could afford them would look much better, and we don't. Still, it felt good.

Tish announced that the next step was "black-head extraction," a cruel-sounding clinical term at odds with her lullaby voice. Thanks to a large, brightly lit magnifying glass that she positioned inches from my nose, Tish found dozens of clogged pores and future blemishes to dig at with her metal tool. I couldn't help but recall an NPR story about how everyone has mites—actual eight-legged arthropods—all over their face and I wondered if her magic magnifier allowed Tish to see mine—eating and mating on my cheeks and chin. Suppressing a gag, I guided my thoughts back to Ravi. And Bruce.

For the next forty minutes, Tish studied my lines and crevices, my age spots and crow's-feet while I wondered what became of old Bruce MacDonald. Tish could see my skin's future and it was headed nowhere good. It was her duty to tell me what was coming, and her pleasure to present products that would help me sidestep that which could be sidestepped.

There are three reasons I'm a poor candidate for high-end potions and lotions like the ones Tish was contractually bound to foist on me. I am cheap. I am lazy. I am impatient. This makes me a fan of microwaved dinners, baseball hats, and the Swiffer.

Before she wasted too much time on me, I felt I should explain to Tish my hang-ups with money.

"I worked in nonprofits for ten years, and my mother was kind of anticonsumerism—" I started to explain the backdrop for my economic policies but petered out. "The thing is, I'm not a spender. I shop but I can never pull the trigger."

Tish nodded. "Tell me more," she said.

Softened by her attentive nature, I expounded, "I have zero willpower. I break promises to myself about seven times a day, even the tiniest promises, like I was going to make my bed every day just as, like, a statement of self-discipline or a daily assertion that I'm in control of *some*thing—and nope."

She nodded. "Go on."

"Well, I'm working on rituals. I think that could help." I shifted so we could see each other more comfortably. "You know, if you put the everyday small things on autopilot and do them without thinking, then you have head space for bigger stuff. Like how Obama wears the same suit every day. One less decision." In every journal of mine going back to 1976, I have outlined my aspiration to be a more regulated person. After many failed attempts at personal overhaul, I had narrowed my goals to one: take a daily shower. Habitual hygiene looked so good on so many women I knew.

"Routines are comforting," Tish said.

"Exactly. So, as for my skin, if I was only going to focus on one thing, I'd want to work on my forehead. I don't need a special mirror to see *those* wrinkles. I see them every day in the car window. Then when I get in the driver's seat, there they are, perfectly isolated in the rearview mirror, making me think there must be someone else in the car with me, someone like my mother." I raised my eyebrows so she could see the full extent of the problem. "It's like an eight-lane highway up there."

She smiled. "Is there anything else you would like to tell me?" I loved her.

34

"Forehead's the big thing. But like I said, I don't use night creams and I buy my makeup at Target. So, given all that, is there *one thing* you can recommend, specifically for my forehead?"

"Bangs."

Oh, Tish, angel-eyed, golden-eared Tish! No one—no hair stylist or waitress, no clerk or cashier, not my spouse and certainly not my children—has listened to me quite so intently, has heard me the way you have. I bless you each time I trim the bangs I've had ever since.

I recently decoupaged an ugly old wooden chest in my bedroom with scraps of art paper and images I cut out of magazines. Twenty feverish minutes later, I could see that I didn't have enough clips to cover the whole thing, but so what? When you were standing directly in front of the trunk and six to eight feet away, it was flawless. Later that afternoon, high on progress, I was discovered in the kitchen creating what *House Beautiful* called *an accent wall*.

Edward, a bore for preparation, frowned at the open paint can on our hardwood floors. "Oh, my God—" he said, as Benjamin Moore Foxy Brown dripped from the grapefruit spoon I had used to pry off the lid.

"This'll take me, like, five minutes. And wait till you see what I did upstairs—"

"Nothing takes five minutes, Kelly. Nothing."

We'd been here before. In a day or two, I'd follow his eye to the unfinished side of the chest or a feathered edge of Foxy Brown along the top of a baseboard. Busted, I would nod through his blah blah blah about *slowing down* or *what painter's tape is for*. He didn't understand the way my projects made me tingle with can-do. He couldn't see that each undertaking I "finished" left me drunk with accomplishment. He'd never be able to appreciate that for a mother, the most elusive, exhilarating buzz was *fixing*.

Sometimes, I feel like I can fix anything—even people, even my children.

Now that the girls are what educators and marketers call young adults, I've heard it suggested that we stand back and let them make mistakes, give them "agency." But no one's seriously recommending we abdicate power to teens, right? I mean, think about it. Their prefrontal cortexes aren't even talking to the rest of their brains. They're slaves to their amygdalas, fighting or taking flight robotically, without the benefit of reason. Fully half of them get boners during calculus.

Beyond the dubious logic of deferring to the teen gut, there's love. The love I know doesn't hang back. My love steps up. I pick up crying babies. I get in bed next to sulking tweens. I read the blogs about growing pains and academic pressure and body image. I stock the medicine cabinet with heating pads, Midol, arch supports. And as they've gotten older and bumped into mean girls, and the meaner parts of themselves, I have hovered nearby, a ready, eager advisor. Why wouldn't I? I lived through it. I have answers. I can save them. If only they would come to me. Which they never do. Unless it's after 10:30 p.m. or I am traveling—like, say, to my twenty-fifth college reunion.

I had just landed at Dulles. Tracy Tuttle, my freshman-year roommate, picked me up.

Though she often says she's 5'11", Tracy is six feet tall and, thanks to her jackrabbit metabolism, lean as Twiggy. She has a great laugh and loves parties, music, and late-night diner food. We initially fell into step with each other because we smoked the same cigarettes and watched the same soap operas—ABC all the way. (By the end of orientation week, although we shared not a single physical feature, Tracy and I were so often together, people started calling both of us Trelly rather than try to work out who was who.)

I threw my roller bag in the back of her minivan and settled in for the two-hour ride to campus, where we would be reminded of inane drinking games, a band called the White Animals that we worshipped to the point of tears, and—thanks to a run-in with the five-year-reunion kids, who invited us to play beer pong and thought we were *adorable*—our age.

Traffic-wise, the area around Dulles is a bitch. Two hours would become four, but we had a full conversational agenda: Tracy was selling her real estate business after twenty years; we had both just seen *Birdman,* so there was that to untangle; and we were mothers. If we used to talk into the night parsing the subtleties of our interactions with the brothers of Lambda Chi, we could talk family dynamics till morning now.

Tracy said she and Tom, her husband, had been arguing lately about when to let your kids start figuring things out on their own. "He's so into them being independent and solving their own problems." Tracy wanted to agree—backing off sounded so good. "But it's impossible. It's like watching them do a puzzle and they're getting so frustrated and you can see the piece they need, it's *right there*. I mean, seriously, how long can you go before you hand it to them? Even though it makes them feel stupid. Even though it takes away all the fun of finishing something on your own."

I admitted that I can't watch the girls climb a tree without telling them where to put their foot next. "I can sit on my hands for about eight seconds. When they tell me about a problem— which is rare and getting rarer—I can think of five things they should do before they finish their first sentence."

"Right. But then, there's that whole weird thing where half the time, it's not even about what they say it's about. So your advice is totally wrong because you don't even understand what the real problem is or what they're asking for."

"Yup." Bangs, not wrinkle cream.

"Lately, I've been trying to get them to just keep talking, to tell me more and more," Tracy said. "I say, *What else?; Go on; Is that all?* And while they're talking, I try really hard not to jump in or cut them off. Like recently, Billy had this coach—"

Hand to God, before she could get into the story, Georgia called, bawling.

Fairly early on, Edward and I had it in our heads that Georgia was the picture of confidence, confident to the point of being argumentative. And in certain circles she was—for example, in the circle that is our family. With us, she was a vocal and often victorious self-advocate. We'd seen none of the classic indicators of trouble. Eating, sleeping, homework? Like a champ.

But at school? In a circle of sixth-grade girls? There, she was getting bounced around, and she didn't like it. So combine my outdated rap on her, kiln-dried when her preschool teacher referred to her as "fierce," with my total lack of access to her school self, and you'll understand why I thought it was a wrong number when I heard an eleven-year-old blubbering into my phone.

"Mommy, Mommy, I hate sixth grade! It's not fair and everyone just lies," she sobbed.

I have to come clean here: something terrible happens to me when my girls cry, more so now than when they were infants and I was able to remind myself that crying was their only method of communication. I didn't like it back then, who does?, but, aided by what Edward dubbed a Red Lobster pour of icy cold sauvignon blanc each evening at five, I managed. Now? Crying that indicates existential pain? The possible onslaught of unhappiness? Isolation, despair? That kind of crying is more threatening to me than a lump in my breast. It's like being skinned alive.

With Tracy beside me, I put Georgia on speaker.

"Everyone's turning on me because they say I was mean to Piper but I wasn't mean to Piper."

You must have said something, I wanted to say. Her school's most recent Life Skills newsletter emphasized Personal Responsibility. Maybe, if I could get her to see her own error, we'd be one step closer to resolution. But Tracy whispered, "Let her get it out."

"Tell me what happened," I said.

"I didn't say anything, even though Piper has been really mean to me like ten times!"

Tracy looked at me with raised eyebrows. "Just say it back to her," she mouthed.

"So everyone's mad at you about being mean to Piper, but you weren't."

"Right!" Georgia said. "And *she* was mean to *me!*"

Tracy nodded. *Do it again.*

"Piper was mean to you and you're getting blamed for being mean to her."

"Yes."

Tracy circled her hand in that unmistakable *Go on* motion, so I said, "What else?"

"Remember at Christmas, when Jackie was mean to Emma?"

I told her I did, though I did not (and could not, at that moment, picture an Emma).

"Nobody got mad at Jackie."

Cyrano de Bergerac fed me another line: "So, no one was mad at Jackie."

"No one!"

How would Edward handle this? I wondered. Not by "wallowing in it," I was sure. His standard course of action was to stifle the drama with a *There, there, you'll be fine,* and then start handing out gum.

Tracy said softly, "That must feel so unfair," which brought to mind my friend Paul, who told me once that at cocktail parties, whenever someone tells him what they do for work he says, *That must be really hard,* and every time, no matter what they do, they say, *Oh, it is.* He started doing it because he's shy and needs the other person to do the talking, but he kept doing it as a public service. Everyone loves Paul; they can't say exactly why, but I think I can.

"That must feel so unfair," I said.

"It does." Georgia's voice was newly steady.

I assumed we had exhausted the facts, but I wanted Tracy to see I was getting it so I asked, "Is there more?"

Georgia practically came through the phone. "Everyone is protecting Piper, but when I need protection, there's nobody! Why isn't anyone standing up for me?"

"That must be awful and confusing, like *Why am I being treated one way and Piper another?*"

"Exactly."

Hitting her blinker, Tracy smiled. I had to admit, asking for more, and listening, was a thousand times easier than coming up with consoling thoughts and next steps.

"Wait, Mommy, where are you right now? Are you in Richmond already?"

"Not yet. Another hour or so. There's a band tonight." I opened a can of Pringles.

"Oh, that's good. I have to go. Have fun with Tracy Tut Tut," she said before hanging up.

"That was kind of incredible," I said, holding out the chips for Tracy.

"You know you're doing it right when you hear *exactly,*" Tracy said. "Now, the trick is doing it every time. Which must not be so easy since otherwise, all therapists' kids would be perfect."

Solving Georgia's problem, which had seemed so generous, was both unlikely and ran the risk of demoralizing her. Empathy was the tonic.

I'd learned something else: her situation, which I had started to dismiss as the usual tween mumbo-jumbo, was interesting, and relatable. I didn't care about Piper and Jackie or whatever happened at Christmas with Emma—but feeling unsupported? The sting of injustice? The search for home, for safety? *That* I understood.

Edward and I once had this great conversation (we've had a few here and there). I was telling him how, when I sit in the front of the cab, which I do sometimes if the road is windy and I'm at risk for car sickness, I often end up hearing great or crazy stuff. Like, on a forty-five-minute ride from Big Sky to the Bozeman airport, I talked to a driver named Matt. He was a park ranger by day and made airport runs in the evenings for extra money to help finance his move to Thailand, where he was going at the end of the year, to take over his in-laws' rubber plantation. Come January, Matt would be managing nine thousand rubber trees west of Bangkok. I asked him if he knew how to farm rubber. "It's nothing. You hammer a tap into the trunk, tie a bucket underneath, and watch the money drip out." When I called Edward from my gate to tell him about my ride, he reminded me of a work dinner, years ago, when he'd sat next to a small older man in a blazer much too big for him. The night did not seem promising. Edward was bored. He had texted me from under the table: *This is brutal*. Then someone mentioned Cambodia. Edward asked the man if he'd ever been to that part of the world. He had, he said flatly. It was the first place he went after several years as a political prisoner in Madagascar—thirty-two months, one cell, rats everywhere. Edward snapped to. One question led to another and Edward discovered that this man he was "stuck with" had been an undefeated boxing and judo champion, filed forty patents, and was suing the Dallas Cowboys for using his retractable roof design without permission. George Clooney had optioned the rights to his life story.

"Makes you wonder what else people might tell you if you just keep asking questions."

The winter my father died was the third worst in Philadelphia's history. It snowed almost sixty inches in two months. I had flown home on Valentine's Day, after what Greenie had self-diagnosed as a torn rotator cuff revealed itself on a PET scan to be metastatic bone cancer.

For the first time in twenty-five years, I arrived at PHL and no one met me at the curb. The cab ride was cold and quiet, except for the final directions. "My house," I said, "is the last one on the street, in the cul-de-sac."

Propped up in a chair by the fire, Greenie was swaddled in a turtleneck, a wool sweater, a jacket, long underwear, sweatpants, two blankets, and, somewhere in all of that, a heating pad whose cord I saw trailing out the back. He weighed 133 pounds, down from close to two hundred at his peak. He was pale, his cheeks deflated, making his high smile seem even more prominent than it had always been. I kissed him many times on his head, smoothing his glossy white hair between each peck, letting the shock pulse through me. I knew he hadn't been able to eat much but I wasn't prepared to be so aware of his skull.

After we got him to bed that night, my mom explained that he came downstairs once a day to sit by his new gas fireplace that turned on with a remote control. She also said his pain was extraordinary—cancer that had begun many years before in his bladder had bloomed in his right shoulder blade and rooted in several spots along his spine. Still, for the four or five hours a day when he was awake, my mom said, he was himself, which is to say, positive.

During that first week, when he wasn't in his spot by the fire, my mom, my brothers, and I cycled in and out of his bedroom, pulling up a chair if he was awake, turning off his light if he had fallen asleep. There was so little to be done, so little that could be done. We watched whatever was on ESPN, even bowling, and talked about Duke basketball, Notre Dame lacrosse, and whether LeBron could hold off the Warriors. I felt lucky that my work and my children were back in California, too far to pull me from him. Edward kept saying, "Stay. We're fine." So I did.

For fourteen days, I cleaned his reading glasses and showed him pictures on my phone, stretching them so he could see the detail hidden in the pixels, which often led us into the catalog of spectacular people he had known—the "all-time greats," as he dubbed them. Listening to him gush about Jock Jankey and Noodles Nolker, it occurred to me that if this newest cancer was going to kill him, he had made good on life's most exquisite promise: he loved and was loved in equal measure.

On one of his final afternoons, I was next to him in bed, under the electric blanket, holding his hand and listening to him breathe. The house was quiet, as were we, until he shook his head. "I blew it, Lovey," he said. For the first time in my life, I was scared to hear what my father would say next. Had he had an affair? Cheated a colleague? Squandered the savings? I was tempted to divert him, but there was Tracy Tuttle in my ear.

"Tell me more, Green Man."

He reverberated with regret. "I should have named a kid after Jack Faber." Jack Faber was my dad's college lacrosse coach. Greenie started his first season at the University of Maryland in 1948, the fall Harry Truman won his second term. Coach Faber had been dead for a decade.

"Greenie—"

"Lovey, he saved me."

My dad's family of eight had enough money to eat and cover the mortgage on a three-bedroom, one-bathroom house on Clearspring Road in Govans, Maryland. My dad's mother made extra money by sewing; Cleta could make a flawless three-piece wool suit with silk lining in a week. Like many women of her day, she kept those earnings in an empty Maxwell House can, as backup for those times when her husband might get carried away at the horse track, or the horse track bar. Still, they didn't have enough for one college tuition, much less six. Greenie's choices out of high school were the same as his brothers': the Army, a construction job, or an athletic scholarship.

"Jack Faber put me through college."

"You gave him your best—high scorer, right? You did okay by Faber."

"No. Not at first. You don't know. I almost lost it, the scholarship. He almost had to pull it. I didn't take it seriously. I didn't *appreciate* it. I was paying too much attention to the Betty Sues. Faber called me to his office and said: 'Corrigan, I'm gonna pull your scholarship.' I said, 'You can't. Please. My mother . . . it'll kill her. I'll do anything.' He told me I had one month to get my grades up. He said, 'Listen now, because

47

here's how you're gonna do it: go to every class, every day. I want you there on time, if not early, sitting in the front row, where the professor can't miss you.' I did exactly what he told me, Lovey. And it worked. Without Faber?" He couldn't articulate what that life would have looked like. "I'll tell you one thing, your mother . . . your mother wouldn't have married some bucktoothed dropout sob story."

I smiled at him, at his double victory, but he was still agitated, pushing matters around in some unsettled part of his mind. "Is there more?"

"I stole the wedding."

"*Your* wedding?"

"Yup." His chin hung low. He took a breath. "Too many groomsmen. Too many toasts to me." He'd married my mother in 1962.

"Dad, I'm sure it was okay." If he had been a careless groom, he had been a caring husband. "I think she's over it, Green." In the last few weeks of his life, I'd taken to making a nickname of his nickname.

"No. We should've had a rehearsal dinner. To get all the Corrigan stuff out of the way. But Hank and Cleta didn't have the money for that. All those speeches got pushed to the wedding day, when the attention should have been on your mother."

Too many toasts? This was heavy on his heart

fifty-three years later, three days before he died? He looked down at his hands. I fought the urge to *There, there* him. He sighed. This wedding business wasn't the whole of it.

"You got something else?" I said.

"Oh, Lovey—" He stopped.

"What is it?"

"Tommy—" His eyes glossed at the memory. Tommy was my mother's brother, whom she adored; he died in his forties, of brain cancer. "I didn't do a good job taking care of your uncle Tommy. Not like I should have. Tommy was a special guy."

I was twelve when Uncle Tommy died. I remember him smiling a lot. He liked pond hockey and had an advanced degree in something or other from Princeton. He brought books for my brothers, novels that he had found entertaining or useful. My mom trusted his opinion on politics, investments, and education. Most of all, Tommy made her happy. She was looser when he was around, easygoing, all ditty, no dirge.

"You know, your mother's father, he was—" Greenie considered. "He was a real hard-ass, a real Harry Hard-Ass." I laughed. There were so many imaginary characters in my father's repertoire: Timmy Thin Skin, Dr. Wacko, the Private School Pukes. "He thought the Corrigans were a bunch of buffoons. But then Tommy—the Golden Child, Mr. Ivy League—he sold me in.

Little by little, he got that whole family on my side, even your grandfather."

"He was great, Uncle Tommy."

"I shoulda gone down there more when he was dying. He liked me. I made him laugh, you know. He liked the whole Corrigan thing."

"Mom always said you guys had fun together."

"I could've gone more, stayed longer. I should've gone once a week." His voice was low, like he was whispering to God, not me. "I owe Tommy a lot. He cleared the way for—" He pointed down the hall to the master bedroom, where my mother slept. Everything referred back to her, his wife, whom he credited with shaping what might have been thin living into an ample life, for all of us.

We rested on that for a while, and then he looked at me, tears filling his eyes.

"Just so you know, Lovey, years later, when the great Father Reinfert was dying—" Father Reinfert was the Corrigan family priest. He married 'em and buried 'em and, in between, baptized every baby he was handed. I didn't know what Father Reinfert had to do with Tommy, but I'd learned to ride out my dad's conversational detours. "I went down to Baltimore and I sat by his bed. I spent a good long afternoon with him. We just talked." He lifted his hands and made them chat to each other like shadow puppets.

"Good for you."

"Yeah, and you know what? After he died, the nun who looked after him—what's her name? I can't remember her name, but she told me: *Your visit meant a lot.*" He turned to face me, his cheeks wet. Voice cracking, he said, "She said it really meant a lot to him, Lovey."

"Of course it did." I leaned into him and whispered, "You're a good man, Greenie," letting the tears fall. "The best."

After a minute, I handed him a tissue. Besides the tears, his nose was dripping again.

"Thanks. I can't—the drip drip never stops." And then a sigh.

"Is there more? You can tell me."

"You know, I guess that's it." The deep creases of agitation between his eyebrows softened. His forehead was smooth again. "I think I'm good, Lovey."

We nodded and squeezed our four hands together, closing every gap.

I Don't Know

I first met Mary Hope, who goes by MH, at swim team practice, in June 1978. I was eleven and though she had a year on me, you wouldn't know it by looking at her chest. Equally flat, shivering in nylon suits, our shoulder straps held together behind our backs with rubber bands, we stood by the starting blocks. She seemed friendly but I hung back. MH was a real swimmer. She wore a swim cap. I had seen her do flip turns and butterfly. I, a lazy breast-stroker, knew my place.

The following summer at YMCA Camp Tockwogh on the Chesapeake Bay, there she was again, waiting in line at the tetherball court in pink corduroy Op shorts. My mother had sent me to camp in a hand-me-down pair of my brother Booker's Jams and at that moment, I hated her for it. MH waved—she even remembered my name—but she was a Ute and I was just a Chickasaw. I smiled and kept walking, not quite in my skin enough to test the pecking order.

Ten years later, I moved to California, where MH was the only person I knew—if you can call swimming in the same pool and going to the same summer camp knowing someone. At first, I only called her if I had a specific question—say where to watch the Blue Angels air show, or get a parking permit. But she was generous about opening her social circle to me, and after a few solid nights getting bombed together on Union Street, we started talking all the time.

Make no mistake, MH was still ahead of me on life's ladder. While I was sleeping through my alarm and eating Froot Loops for dinner, she worked at Autodesk and had a 401K. She lived with her fiancé, a suave motorcycle-riding Russian named Leon. She owned a coat rack and a file cabinet. She waxed her eyebrows and was in a book club. I remember watching her cook one Saturday night, casually drizzling olive oil over salmon steaks while talking about an "off-site" in Carmel, and thinking that she had more personal authority than anyone I'd ever known. MH was twenty-eight.

Several years passed. At the same time that Edward and I were falling in love, she and Leon were gearing up to start a family. From our cubicles across town, we whispered bits of news to each other over the phone.

"I'm going home with him for Thanksgiving," I said.

"We went off the pill," she said.

"He's moving in."

"My period is ten days late."

"We're engaged!"

"We're pregnant!"

It was the summer of 2000. The genome was

being mapped, Elián González was reunited with his father in Cuba, Al Gore was going to be president, I was a newlywed and MH was a young, upwardly mobile professional hustling around San Francisco with a life-changing secret. Life was behaving all around.

Toward the end of her first trimester, one week after she saw her baby's outline in black and white for the first time, MH started spotting. She rushed to see her doctor. No heartbeat. A D and C was scheduled to remove "the contents of the uterus." Life had stopped complying.

Her ob-gyn told MH her eggs were "not great," but even so, she was able to get pregnant a second time. That pregnancy ended with another D and C shortly after MH heard the heartbeat. A second doctor explained to MH that she was that "rare case" where both getting pregnant and staying pregnant were fraught. Still, six months after her second D and C, she managed to get pregnant a third time. She told almost no one. Ten weeks in, she heard a heartbeat and we celebrated cautiously on the phone. "This is the one," I said. Eight days later, the ultrasound wand crossed her belly in grave silence. Her doctor saw so many women with fertility issues that when MH showed up for her third D and C, he didn't even recognize her.

"I feel like it's my fault," she said while we drank tea on her back stoop in Marin, throwing a tennis ball for her dog. "No matter what I do, I'm not healthy enough." She had stopped drinking alcohol, walked an hour a day, slept eight hours a night. She went to acupuncture and got weekly massages. She showed me red marks on her back from something called cupping that was supposed to improve something called Qi. She passed on a promotion. Finally, to eliminate all possible stress, she took a leave of absence from work. None of it mattered. "Nothing works and no one can tell me why."

Four years into her pursuit of motherhood, MH met with a new doctor, a woman, who listened to the whole story and then said, "I want to say something before we get into your medical options: You have permission to stop. No one will call you a quitter." That was the turning point. "That one comment, that we had permission to stop, made room for us to think about other options," MH said. That's when she and Leon stopped asking *why* and started looking at alternatives.

They considered egg donation. At an early appointment, she was handed a bulging catalog of donors to flip through. She had no idea how to think about the selection process. "I mean, every egg donor is in pristine health, that's a given. So, I'm looking at all this other stuff. Should I pick someone who looks like me? Or someone I *wished* I looked like? Should I consider where they went to college, who had the highest SAT scores, what varsity sports they played? Because it's all there." After a long weekend in Napa, many deep breaths, and some counseling, they chose to pursue adoption.

An adoption attorney told MH that step one was to create a "Why you?" brochure, a four-page color advertisement that would be sent to teen pregnancy clinics, inner-city hospitals, and Christian sororities across the United States. I took a couple hundred shots of MH and Leon—arm in arm, on their stoop, making pancakes, walking their dog—and acted as one of several editors helping them jam their entire lives into six winning paragraphs. *We eat organic and exercise regularly. We have nice parents and good educations and a spare bedroom that will make a beautiful nursery. We value travel and family time and reading. We work hard but not too hard.* At the bottom of each page was an 800-number, in bold, that went straight to MH's cellphone. While Leon picked up eleven boxes of pamphlets at Kinko's, we stamped and addressed six hundred manila envelopes.

The calls started coming: calls from teenagers who weren't really pregnant, calls from teenagers who were pregnant and asked for money, calls from couples, like the high school sweethearts in Modesto who asked MH to take them to Denny's for dinner and then emailed later to say they had decided to keep the baby.

Two years later, after Georgia and Claire had arrived, MH got a call from a hospital in northern California. It was a Sunday afternoon and she was packing for a work trip to Germany. A baby girl had been born. Her biological mother had met with a social worker and reviewed a binder full of brochures representing eager prospective parents. The mom picked MH and Leon. They would never know why. "It was unreal," MH said. "I couldn't understand what was happening."

When MH and Leon entered the NICU, a nurse named Carol in floral scrubs and red clogs looked up at MH and then back down at the baby in her arms and said, with a lilt in her voice, "There's Mommy. There she is. There's Mommy." Carol found a private room where MH and Leon could hold their daughter for the first time. Shaking with disbelief and wonder, MH told me later she just kept saying *Hi . . . hi.*

The first time I held Eliza, she was two weeks old.

I fawned and marveled and tried out different words: Eliza was *an angel, a wonder, a bit of perfection in a muddy world.* When her binky popped out, she let out a screech I knew well from Claire. MH laughed as she slipped the pacifier back between Eliza's lips. "I don't know who this kid is," MH said, "but so far, I can tell you she knows how to get what she wants."

"I don't know who this kid is"? Georgia hadn't

clocked a full day on earth before we started ascribing her features and behaviors to various family members. Declarations in the maternity ward about her mother's eyes and her father's long toes were a predictable and innocent part of the euphoria, and a way to demystify the mystery before us. We were laying claim to the child we had made. She was ours, and every bit of her was a possible reference to someone in our tribe. Two weeks in, we said knowing things like *She's a smartie, this one* and *She loves being clean.*

But MH hadn't become a mother over the course of nine months. She hadn't rubbed her belly a thousand times, *foreseeing* her child. She hadn't looked for her mother's deep dimple in Eliza's cheek or hoped her child would inherit her husband's mind for math. MH and Leon had accepted the call to raise a child, not by railroading her into becoming a gratifying mashup of biology and dreams, but by allowing her to reveal her nature over time, in no particular order, with switchbacks and reversals along the way.

Twelve years later, MH still says, "I don't know who this kid is." Now she adds, "But she does. She knows exactly who she is. I'm just along for the ride."

I don't know is a fairly humble position to take as a parent—humble, and astute. Me, I can't do it. I latch on to some idea about who my girls are and who that means they'll be and boy, I do not like it when they evolve or change. God help the kid who loves scavenger hunts and tag and sing-alongs and then becomes hesitant to join in all the reindeer games. Who plays three sports and then quits them all to try on makeup with her new friends Imogen and Jetta at the mall. Who likes boys and then likes girls. Edward reminds me that I once seemed genuinely betrayed when Georgia changed her mind about hummus. *But you told me you loved hummus!*

Growing up, my brothers were the athletes of the family. They were good at everything: ice hockey, touch football, golf, lacrosse, as well as all quasi-sports like darts, bowling, billiards, keep-it-up. I was one of two girls cut from cheerleading even though my voice can be heard from a city block away and the Radnor Raiders white sweater would have sat nicely on what some kid at my bus stop once called my *power rack*. That's the moment I turned my back on sports and cultivated the artsy identity that I've clung to ever since.

Recently, a fellow creative came to see me in California. Anna and I liked each other for many reasons, one of which—I thought—was that we both saw clearly that it was either the life of the mind or the life of the body, never both. We talked contemporary fiction like some people talked target heart rates. But then, while

I wasn't looking, Anna had found herself a personal trainer. (Traitor.) After a year of planks and something called burpees, she had Michelle Obama arms and could wear anything, even dresses made of *Lycra*.

"Man, I wish I had that gene," I said, the unfashionable slope of my shoulders safely hidden inside a structured jacket that probably aged me a decade.

Anna laughed. "That's just a story you tell yourself."

I nodded deeply, slowly, like I was really taking that idea in, while thinking, *What the hell is she talking about?* Was she trying to say I was choosing a life of lumps? That my BMI wasn't a foregone conclusion? Pfft.

Turns out, I'm a whiz at simplifying complicated matters. The dissolution of a twenty-year marriage that might take a decade of therapy to deconstruct? Not for me. My friend's ex was a *narcissist and degenerate* and she, *a total catch*. I can reduce the troubling state of our democracy to a single Supreme Court case. I hear myself promoting all the usual notions: teachers are self-sacrificing saints, administrators are bureaucratic and out of touch, women apologize too much, men mansplain, moms nurture (as they multitask), dads grill and take out the trash and think "everything's fine." And don't get me going on cat people.

My only comfort: I'm not the only one who likes a label.

When I had cancer, *a lot* of people ascribed *a lot* of admirable qualities to me. The long story is the subject of another book but at thirty-six, I found a seven-centimeter tumor in my breast while taking a bath. A week after my biopsy, I sat in a mauve recliner for eight hours hooked up to the mother of all chemotherapies: Adriamycin. Ten days later, my hair was gone. Bald, with two kids in diapers, I was an announcement no one wanted to hear: disease happens, suddenly and unbidden.

After a few weeks, Edward and I both noticed something. Every conversation fell into the same pattern. Cancer was The Enemy, treatment was A Journey, and I was A Hero whose responsibility was to weather the shipwrecks and beat back the sea monsters, returning from the odyssey changed and better. It was uncanny how many people said one or more of these three things: *You're so brave. Was it in your family?* and *What a wake-up call.*

Brave? The first time I saw my name on a gurney, I burst into tears like a toddler running from a bee. After a forty-five-minute outpatient surgery to stitch a port just below my collarbone so nurses could flood my bloodstream with a variety of chemotherapies, I overheard the surgeon characterize me to Edward as "very emotional." I cheered at the sight of the signs around the hospital that said: *Pain is not required. Let us help!* I took a dozen pills a day: pills to soften stool, lower anxiety, and aid sleep; pills to quell mouth sores, quiet bone pain, and reduce nausea. Whatever could be pharmacologically eased, I pharmacologically eased.

As for the genetic element, I could tell people were hoping it ran in my family—I suspect because if the bum genes didn't run in theirs, that meant they were safe. But I was, like almost 90 percent of breast cancer patients, a spontaneously occurring mystery, and who wants to read that headline every day?

Though it would've been a pleasing end of the story to claim that cancer reprioritized my life, I didn't need *a wake-up call.* Having worked for nonprofits for ten years, I was wide awake. Spend part of every week touring middle managers from Citibank around San Francisco's Tenderloin transitional housing, and your sheets start to feel real soft. As for my marriage, I suppressed panic attacks about my singledom during *twenty-four* weddings. I pined for him, whoever he was. I still reach across at night to touch the side of Edward's body, just to be sure it really worked out. My children? I internalized the stories of MH and three other friends who navigated endometriosis, ectopic pregnancies, polycystic ovaries, lazy sperm, and sperm that swam in circles. When I peed on that stick and the line appeared, I held it to my chest and wept. But who can blame people for trying to make sense of a young mom with Stage 3 disease?

After trying a few different comebacks to *You're so brave* and *What a wake-up call,* I found the best answer was *Into every life, some rain must fall.* Between you and me, though, I'm pretty sure the cancer thing was my fault. I smoked for thirteen years and drank like I was in college for a decade after I graduated. Even after the word was out, I ate meat and dairy loaded with growth hormones, and leftovers microwaved in plastic containers. I took down three Diet Cokes a day and sweetened my coffee with whatever the global corporations put in those pastel packets on café tables. I still have a Buddha belly, even though many health organizations have released statements detailing the sobering correlation between abdominal fat and cancer, and willfully disregard what I know about exercise—fifteen minutes on the treadmill at Level 1 is the recommendation of exactly zero doctors.

See how this works? I made bad choices, I got sick; I make better choices, I stay well.

There *are* exceptional people who can live with the complexity of things, who are at peace with the unknown and the unknowable. I love these people. I feel safe with them in a way that I never could with the men and women of resounding conviction, even though in the game of influencing people, saying *I'm not sure* or *Sort of* is about as winning as body odor. (Remember *Fast Times at Ridgemont High,* when Mr. Hand destroys Spicoli for admitting he doesn't know why he does the things he does?) Why we don't value intellectual honesty over easy answers is beyond me. I'm just saying there are no inspirational management posters celebrating STILL THINKING and I've had long arguments with Edward that come down to this: someone changed their mind and the other person didn't like it one bit.

Beyond my low-grade addiction to the pleasure of feeling sure is the niggling sense that I'm supposed to know. According to my ballot, the state of California wants my opinion on the future of affirmative action and high-capacity magazine weapons. And why wouldn't they? I have degrees from accredited institutions. The Bank of America trusted me with a thirty-year mortgage and Alta Bates Medical Center sent me home, twice, with helpless infants who became teenagers who want answers and *from me.*

My friend Sarah is a loving, petite brainiac who has to rise high on her toes to land the good hugs she insists on giving. She skipped seventh grade, went to Harvard at seventeen, and, because she cottons to science and children, became a pediatrician. She's seen it all. In my small family alone, she's diagnosed meningitis, pneumonia, vertigo, and a gnarly peritonsillar abscess that required lancing.

Over dark coffee and morning buns at our regular spot, Sarah told me about an appointment the day before with a favorite patient. She can't use names, of course, so she calls all boys Sam. This "Sam" was a fourth-grader. He had a horsey laugh and said thank you a lot. "Mom," as Sarah called her, brought him in because his math teacher said he had been disruptive lately. Mom had noticed that Sam was a slow reader and had a hard time following directions. Mom went to WebMD and Healthline and a site called Totally ADD. Not surprisingly, Mom was convinced Sam totally had ADD.

"I got in the examination room with Sam, and Mom was raring for a diagnosis," Sarah said. "Her nephew had gone on Ritalin and it was really working for him." Sarah has her own children; she understands the need to know, and fast. "She wanted a plan and I couldn't give it to her. I couldn't say what was going on with Sam. Maybe it was a stage. Maybe he hated math, or his math teacher, or the kid sitting next to him. Mom was so frustrated—with the situation but also with me. It was almost like she *wanted* her son to have a disorder, or even walk out with a misdiagnosis, like that would have been better."

Sarah said the biggest change in her practice is finally feeling okay saying *I don't know* and dealing with the parents' predictable, understandable disappointment. "I mean, they want answers—they're ready to take action—and the web always has an answer. Telling parents who spent the weekend online convincing themselves of a diagnosis that you're *not sure* or you *need more information . . .*" She shrugged. "But you have to, you have to take the time to ask the right questions, think it through, keep collecting information."

In Sarah's first year as an M.D., her practice saw its one and only case of SIDS. The baby, a third child, was four months old when she died during naptime on her first afternoon of daycare. "I went to visit the family at home the week after," she said. "They had so many questions. There are things that make SIDS more likely: mothers under twenty, mothers who smoke, children who are multiples. But none of that was the case for this mom, this family." She stopped to shake her head at the memory. "It's the same with suicide, when they don't leave a note," Sarah said, giving me a shiver. "At some point, it doesn't matter why. The family has to stop asking questions and face the grief. Getting to that place can take a very long time."

My cousin Kathy came to mind. Her son, Aaron, was killed in a car accident; he got in the wrong car on the wrong night. Kathy had been with him earlier that evening. He was planning to swing by a party after dinner. She didn't like the look of the skies. The roads would be slick. She tried to keep him with her, laid on the charm and good humor, two of her strongest suits. *Come home with your momma, those fools will be around tomorrow, we can watch a movie, I'll make popcorn. . . .* But Aaron was *just going for a bit. . . .*

"For maybe ten years," she told me, "I kept asking, *Why did this happen?* It was all I could think about some days." She said she tried a dozen different stories, but nothing fit. Nothing stuck. Until she finally figured it out: It happened because it can. Cars can flip. They can skid out and turn over and hit a tree. The metal can bend, the glass can break, the roof can cave in. It's a car, it's a body, physical objects with physical properties that obey the physical world. Seeing that clearly, embracing that unadulterated reality, rearranged her insides, making it easier, finally, to breathe.

There are questions and there are Questions. On the matter of God, I've stood in every square on the board: obedient believer, secretly hopeful, open-but-dubious. I've walked away from the board entirely, only to circle back. Today, all I can say is: I don't know what I think about God, either the one who was presented to me from behind the marble altar during my childhood or the many God-like ideas that have been offered to me since. I do know that I love many believers and I pulse with gratitude that wants a locus and I wonder about the wonders I see around me and feel inside me. But I'm not sure of anything. I don't *know,* not like my parents.

They both grew up in 1940s Baltimore, where doubt either didn't exist or was not discussed. Fish on Fridays, the inevitable sainthood of Mother Teresa, the dazzling promise of heaven, where you get to be with all your favorite people forever—done, done, and done.

"Lovey, what can I tell you? It was a simpler time," my dad said once when I asked him about the family faith. "Everyone we knew was Catholic. We were surrounded by believers."

"We wouldn't have dared question it," added my mom. "And we didn't want to."

As a child, I operated comfortably enough within Catholicism. Sure, there were words I said in mass—hallowed, apostolic, trespassed—that I didn't understand. Yes, I was confused about whether *Hosanna* referred to Jesus or God or some third figure who was also due a measure of worship. And for sure, I was peeved that my brothers were trusted to transport miniature glass pitchers of holy water to the priest while girls, dumb and klutzy, were confined to the pews.

But I loved the taste of Communion, the smell of incense, the sound of the organ, the part when we all shook hands and said "Peace be with you." And, well, boys went to church.

The best ones went to 11:15 a.m. mass at St. Katherine's. Squat and brick, St. Kitty's, as we called it, sat on a corner in Wayne surrounded by gas stations. Inside, the altar was not at one end but in the center, which meant I could scan the crowd section by section for Charlie Ryan, Andy Sheehan, and the deadly cute Kenny Graves. Thick brown hair with honey highlights, rosy cheeks, the perfect mole near his sly smile, the best one-liners: Kenny was too much. His older sister, Leslie, was a favorite of the Brothers Corrigan, so I could often follow GT or Booker's gaze to find my reward. I spent the service stealing glances and coordinating my arrival at the altar with his. Once there, I stuck my tongue out and lowered my head modestly, hoping to trick Pure and Good Kenny into thinking a different brand of thoughts.

Other than mass—weekly for my brothers and me, daily for my parents—Catholicism made two other claims on us: Lent and Confession. Every spring, in addition to making some Lenten sacrifice, my mother would lead us on an hour-long tour around the inner perimeter of the church to absorb the story of Jesus's death and resurrection as depicted on fourteen carved marble tableaus called the Stations of the Cross. "This is what happened," she would say, as if the tablets were certain as court records.

As for Confession, I didn't look forward to it, but there was something reassuring about handing myself over to an authority who knew right from wrong and could deliver me from evil. Inside the booth, my standard confession was cursing and taking money from my dad's wallet, after which Father Pat would assign two Hail Marys and three Our Fathers. For the low price of mindlessly reciting prayers in my head, my moral account was reconciled. My brother GT chose to confess face-to-face. That meant he'd actually sit across from the Father in a folding metal chair and look right into his eyes while he itemized the commandments he'd broken since last they talked. I couldn't imagine what GT was saying, but his personal interaction indicated a certainty of belief that I knew I did not have. I remember opening a leather-bound Bible in the pew to a page where Adam was said to have lived for 530 years, and rolling my eyes. How many Hail Marys would I be charged for rolling my eyes at the Holy Bible?

I often asked my dad what he liked about being Catholic; it was important for me to understand. "I'll tell you," he'd say. "I like how hard it is, how much it asks of us. Nobody else has Confession, Lovey. Nobody else has mass every day. You know how many pastors and rabbis would kill to get a congregation to show up every day?" I told him I hoped none. He laughed. "I'm just saying, daily mass is a high bar. That's a special deal."

Once I got to college, there was no time for mass. Sunday mornings were swallowed whole by the Saturday-night recap that began in our dorm room and carried us through a protracted brunch of hush puppies and sheet cake followed by a recuperative afternoon of Diet Cokes and Twix bars on the library hill in boxer shorts and fraternity sweatshirts. During freshman year, I got a letter from my grandmother that said if I was ever sad or confused, I should talk to Jesus like he was my "best friend." I showed the note to Tracy Tuttle, my human best friend. We laughed and said we could talk to each other but still, I kept the letter. I liked thinking that between Jesus, my grandmother, and Tracy, *someone* had my back.

Toward the end of junior year, I surprised myself (and Tracy) by slipping away from our Sunday dinners to attend the last mass of the day. It was the only thing I did on campus by myself.

For the hour between dinner and my mandatory sorority meeting—where agendas included critical matters like "Intramural jerseys: magenta with aqua, or aqua with magenta?"—I stepped into a high-ceilinged space and got small. I loved it, not the talk of Jesus but the incense, the organ, the sharing of peace. I loved completing the motions of mass from muscle memory. Maybe my religion was nostalgia. As I crossed campus after the service, I felt both independent and lulled by the exquisite internal music that accompanies the habits of childhood. I suppose I was starting the fabled "return to family" they say happens around that time.

A decade later—a decade that involved non-profit work, nannying abroad, night school, and precious little religious activity—Edward and I were planning our wedding. Though we toyed with marrying in a meadow at Yosemite, I knew we would end up at St. Thomas, a 150-year-old dual-spired chapel half a mile from my childhood home on Wooded Lane. In order to secure the date, we were required to complete something called Pre-Cana, a guided period of premarital reflection about finances, cohabitation, in-laws, faith, and fifteen other subjects. The process began with a bubble test. One hundred and sixty statements that we were to agree or disagree with. *I trust my future spouse. Pornography is acceptable in our marriage. My future spouse's family interferes with our relationship.*

After our questionnaires had been compared, we reported to a modest office below St. Mary's Cathedral in San Francisco to discuss every statement where our responses diverged, a conversation that took twenty hours of counseling to complete. Guiding us through it all was a seventy-something monsignor named John O'Connor who looked a lot like Steve Martin. He brought us snickerdoodles on a paper plate and mint tea in foam cups. He laughed at my nervous jokes. He was humble and earnest, reiterating his inexperience with marriage while reminding us that he had counseled many hundreds of couples over the last fifty years. We couldn't know the future, was his refrain, but we could learn how to know each other—*or rather keep knowing each other,* and that would keep our union safe. I loved him and felt loved by him. The church was invested in the health of our marriage and I was grateful for it.

At our wedding the following April, the toast began with Uncle Jimmy, the tallest and most eloquent of the Originals, as my cousin Kathy dubbed my dad and his siblings. Jimmy said a few kind things about the reception, looking at my mother, and then turned to Edward to say he hoped he was a better husband than he was a golfer. My brothers layered on some cracks about mulligans. Then Uncle Jimmy came to his point, which I assumed would be about God but was instead about respect for the unknown.

"I don't know if you caught it in the homily but—Hold on, I have it right here," he said, fishing around in his breast pocket for a note he'd scribbled during the ceremony. "Did you hear what the padre said? He said: *Life is a mystery to be lived.* Now I'm an old guy and I've seen a lot and that's really true. Life is a mystery to be lived. So, Edward, Kelly, here's to your mystery."

Nothing reveals beliefs like crisis. The same fall that I was diagnosed with breast cancer, my dad was diagnosed with bladder cancer. My father got his diagnosis in person; after scheduling a slew of tests and thanking the doctor, he and my mother drove to their favorite Main Line chapel, St. Colman's. My ob-gyn gave us my biopsy results over the phone. I let Edward hold me for a long time, then we had a Corona on the deck. After that, we opened our laptops searching for information on invasive ductal carcinoma. They gave it to God; we gave it to Google.

Greenie's cancer and mine were both Stage 3, but he was sicker. The location of the lesions around his bladder, combined with his age, made his case more complicated and less hopeful. One of his doctors told GT in confidence that we should "enjoy this year with him." We couldn't imagine Greenie dying. We couldn't even imagine him spending a day in bed. He seemed too vital to die. And I suppose he was, because nine months later, after two surgeries and a chemo-radiation combo, Greenie was body-surfing at the Jersey shore and talking about playing pond hockey that next winter.

It was miraculous, people said. At the very least, it was unexpected. Perhaps even unexplainable, though not to my mom, who knew precisely how to account for her husband's recovery. "People around the world were praying for your father," she explained—"around the world" referring primarily to my friend Charlie who lived in Moscow and had always been fond of my dad. But I hadn't prayed for Greenie. I didn't believe in God enough to submit a request and didn't want to be—to borrow from sixth-grade parlance—a *user* who thought she could get what she wanted by conveniently nuzzling up to someone she usually snubbed.

After my dad recovered, I talked to Tracy Tuttle about my parents' confidence in prayer and their belief that God had intervened on their behalf. Tracy was not surprised but she didn't agree, either. Rather than praise the inexplicable glory of God, she said, couldn't we exalt the ingenuity of man? "Isn't it weird how people want to give all the credit away, as if we were useless, as if we had no idea how to take care of ourselves or each other?" In other words, maybe it wasn't prayer that made Greenie better—maybe it was the scope with tiny scissors that engineers created and doctors manipulated to remove nine tumors from his bladder. Or all that chemo. Or the doctor who managed his case with vigilance. I liked Tracy's take on things: up with people and their hard work and cool inventions.

But then, I remembered the urologist who had told us to brace for the worst. Ten months later, when he declared my father a healthy man, that same doctor said he couldn't explain "how on earth" my dad was disease-free. Could I really glorify a doctor who shrugged his shoulders and said my dad's survival was "anybody's guess"? And between those two poles lay a dozen other possibilities.

At this very moment, it's a decent bet that my mom is praying for me and my brothers, who she hopes will inherit her bulletproof faith but are more likely to drive away with her navy Buick and a leftover case of Chardonnay she bought at a discount over the state line in Delaware. "I'm telling you, Kelly," she has said to me a couple hundred times, "prayer is powerful. You should try it." The closest I come to prayer is to give a nod of thanks for a just-right avocado or an ache that's resolved or a five-star public school teacher like Ms. McKuen. At night, after I get in bed and pull my covers around me, I sometimes think, "Thank you for this good man beside me and those girls in the other room." I have no specific ideas about who "you" is.

In cafés around Berkeley and Oakland,

community bulletin boards scream with beliefs—
Tantra! Chi Nei! Beading Meditation! There
are ads for weekend seminars where you can
make your passion canvas, your soul collage,
your purpose manifesto. I once saw a stack of
glossy cards promoting the International Clitoris
Festival, praise be to that. When I go home to
Philly, I see gold crosses around the necks of
my high school friends and drive past sandwich
boards telling me to sign my kids up for Bible
camp. I'm wont to dismiss it all as so much
yearning but really, who am I to say? What if
there *is* something between and around and
inside of all seven billion of us? As Voltaire said:
"Doubt is not a pleasant condition, but certainty
is absurd."

When the girls ask me about God, I say that
people believe all kinds of things and no one
really knows, including me, but that I hope for
God. I tell them that there are things that exist—
six hundred different varieties of ranunculus,
child prodigies, altruism—that are so riddled
with mystery I have to wonder. Edward tells them
that being a parent has been the most spiritual
experience of his life—he can't explain why.
"You'll see," he says.

Over the years, the girls have occasionally
wanted to talk about what happens when people
die. I tell them some people think they go to a
paradise, a separate plane of existence where

God holds them in the palm of his hand. Other people say the dead are internalized in the people left behind. Edward says they become part of the earth and therefore, an endless part of the cycle of life. "If you'd asked Greenie," Edward says, "he'd have told you that heaven exists and *boy are you gonna love it*." Just like if you'd asked him why I got better, he'd have said something about how God wanted me to be here, that He had big plans for me. When I told Greenie I got better because there was an antidote, namely four chemotherapies, he just laughed and flashed his big knowing smile. "Aw, Lovey," he said, "don't you see? What do you think makes a man want to spend his days trying to cure cancer?"

That's what stops me from pushing aside the idea of God once and for all. If we're just fancy animals or an accident between ice ages, where does our desire to do good and be good come from? Maybe it's the social contract. Maybe it's reincarnation or Freud's superego. Don't ask me. Any certainty I pretend is a performance to keep the troops calm and in line. Alone in the campaign tent, with maps spread out on the folding table, I work in pencil with shaky hands.

I don't know why MH couldn't carry a baby to term or how she became the choice of that biological mother in northern California paging through couples in the "Why You?" binder. Maybe she liked dogs or thought Leon's Russian childhood was interesting? Maybe she saw something—a readiness—in MH's posture, her eyes? I don't know what I'm doing now that my daughters will later need to undo, what future struggles my parenting is producing. I don't know why I slept well last night and was up for an hour and a half the night before. I don't know how long it will be before I'm back in a hospital and I don't know whether I'll be in the bed or sitting next to it. I don't know if Edward's startup is going to explode or implode. I don't know if all the legislation I so instinctively support—gun control, increased teacher pay, free contraception—would actually solve the problems I'm worried about.

I try to be one of the exceptional people who can live with the complexity of things, who are at peace with the unknown and the unknowable, who leave all the cages open. I tell myself: *There's so much that you don't know, you can't know, you aren't ever going to know.* I beg myself to stop forcing narratives. I remind myself, repeatedly, that real life doesn't conform—or it does, bending perfectly to your idea of what is right and fair and good, leading you to believe (again) in a logic that will later unravel.

Do your work, I tell myself. And after? *Find a patch of lawn and sit down and hug your knees to your chest and let everything you've ever been told and everything you've ever seen mingle together in a show just for you, your own eye-popping pageant of existence, your own twelve-thousand-line epic poem. The tickle of the grass on your thighs, the sky moving over you, sunless or blue, echoes from a homily or a wedding toast or a letter your grandmother sent. Remember something good, a sunburn you liked the feeling of, a plate of homemade pasta. Do your work, Kelly. Then lean back. Rest from the striving to reduce. Like the padre said, life is a mystery to be lived. Live your mystery.*

I Know

I can't tell you any more until I tell you about my friend Liz. It took me fifteen years to really get to know her, but once I did, she reshaped how I feel about my life.

I met her at a club in San Francisco, back in the late nineties when Edward and I did sexy things like go to clubs in San Francisco. A fifteen-piece funk band called Super Booty was playing seventies hits like "Ladies Night" and "Give It to Me Baby." Liz came in on the arm of Andy, Edward's best friend. Tall and willow thin in a sequin minidress, I appreciated her style immediately; anyone would. She inhabited herself with ease. She and Andy were up from Encinitas for a wedding. When the reception petered out, they hailed a cab and beat it down Broadway to meet Edward's new girlfriend.

I sensed immediately that Liz felt protective of Edward. For three years, she'd been his go-to on matters requiring a woman's point of view. They had road-tripped to Tahoe, spending days on the mountain and nights at a cheap roadside casino called the Crystal Cave, where they'd lost and won with a blackjack dealer named Ernest. They'd debated politics and feminism over pitchers of Anchor Steam at The Dutch Goose.

She'd opined about every hookup and hot date. She wasn't going to sign off on *the new girl* without some due diligence.

Unfortunately, I didn't show well that night. I may have had three too many cosmos—they went down so quickly, what with all the ice, and back then I approached every Saturday like it was my last. Also, I was in a stupid outfit. Specifically, I had one of those mini backpacks on. It was on super sale at Nine West and, every time I put it on, I worried that the reason they were giving them away was because the backpack compartment was too small, like *laughably* small, like *is that a deck of cards you have hanging off your shoulders?* small. Also, I may not be the coolest dancer. As these things go, our first meeting wasn't ideal.

At brunch the next morning, while I caffeinated myself through a Level 5 hangover and the boys discussed something called the EBITDA of Andy's startup, Liz and I talked about the East Coast versus the West Coast (she too had lived in both places) and grad school. I had a master's in English literature from San Francisco State and she had a master's in public policy from Duke. She was smart and informed; there was hardly anything I could think to say that would impress or surprise her. As the waitress set a stack of French toast on the table, something came up about health care. As Liz took up the topic, I nodded along as if I was well aware of the coverage problems in rural areas. I'd never heard the term *HMO* and didn't know the difference, or if there was one, between Medicare and Medi-Cal. Edward jumped in with something about Reagan circulating the idea that socialized medicine was the beginning of socialism itself. I left the diner full, and a little intimidated by both her public policy chops and her sisterly rapport with Edward. Before we parted ways, frantic to make an impression, any impression, I told her the one joke I knew, about a kid catching her mother schtupping the piano tuner, and she laughed hard.

As it became clear that Edward and I were in it for life, as were Edward and Andy, so were Liz and I. We spent a few long weekends with them, mostly at other people's weddings. I continued to admire her style and her range; she had Linda Evangelista's capacity for variation. Any hair color or cut seemed to work—blond to her shoulders, brown and cropped tight. I continued to say too much to her too little. But she laughed, and I liked her laugh. And she was smitten with Andy in a girlish way that struck me as endearing. Beyond that, even after several years, I wasn't sure if our friendship had much potential.

Having grown up in a family of extroverts and charisma junkies, I found Liz's choice of smallness curious, maybe even strange. She listened more than she talked, asking questions less to understand herself than to help you refine your own point of view. Andy, who would have fit right in with the Corrigans, had a conversational style that was more familiar. Plus, he had great stories. Nixon, the sports watch company he had started, was taking off and none of us, Liz included, could get enough of the details. Would Tony Hawk agree to endorse Nixon? When would they start to make watches for scuba divers? How were sales in Europe?

After five years, here's what I could tell you about Liz: she was undaunted by cross-country holiday travel or hitting the grocery store at prime time with three kids in tow or surfing in January. Only once did I see *her* hungover. And she had a certain kinetic elegance. She didn't flop down on the sofa; she lowered herself. She didn't clang pots; she lifted them out of drawers and set them on the stovetop. She could weave in and out of a game of tag or catch a falling marker or toss a rotten grape into the sink from across the room. Sometimes when I am missing her, I try to move like she did, even if I'm just unpacking groceries.

With four toddlers in tow, two girls each, our families started vacationing together— Mexico, Colorado, Montana, Arizona. Liz left the planning of adult activities to Andy and me, whose concerns were squarely centered on happy hours and poker. Her attention revolved around the kids—accommodating naptimes and making sure we could find food they'd actually eat.

I watched her at group dinners and wondered what she really thought about things. Cleaning dishes after, we'd talk mommy talk—how to find the right academic environment for each of our kids, or whether that was grossly overthinking it and we should just drop them off at the closest public school, like our parents did. We'd discuss our husbands, their work and what we thought would happen next in their careers. She'd tell me about books she was reading and political campaigns she was tracking. But the stuff of love and anguish? Marital tension and family dysfunction? Not a peep.

When her son Dru, her third and last child, was barely a year old, she felt a strange and persistent pain in her abdomen during yoga. After a few months, her best friend Jessica insisted she see a doctor, which led to an MRI that showed a 13-centimeter tumor on her ovary, and she never got better. She fought in various states for almost seven years. Twenty-five doctors. Twenty-three scans. Four surgeries. Two clinical trials. Eighty-eight rounds of chemotherapy. *Eighty-eight.* And one dose of ketamine from a compassionate therapist who believed, correctly as it turned out, that an afternoon in an altered state might offer some insight and serenity as she began to die.

One morning when we were down visiting, I asked to go to chemo with her and she let me. We packed a bag of magazines, some water, a soft hat. We rode over to the infusion center in her minivan listening to the Foo Fighters. When we got there, she introduced me to everyone, like my father always did. Jen at the front desk, Tara on the floor. We settled into her favorite spot, by the window. A nurse named Jerry came by with her lab results; her white blood cell count looked good. Liz told me Jerry was getting married in three weeks and asked him about his ongoing spat with the caterer. She was a different version of herself there—less in service, more in charge. I told her on the way home that she reminded me of Greenie, the way she related to the staff. Tracking her blood protein and tumor markers could have dominated the appointment, but she didn't let it. The nurses were still interesting to her—she reveled in their lives, their plans for their bright futures.

Maybe a year later, we went again. She was still the youngest patient in the room. After the paperwork was signed and her infusion had begun, she rolled her head across the top of her La-Z-Boy to look at me. "Don't tell Andy, but I don't think this is working, Kelly." While I swallowed that, she asked Jerry how married life was treating him. That was the first big secret she ever told me.

We had seven Thanksgivings together. Our last kicked off the same way the previous six had: with cocktails and an original production written and performed by our five kids. The 2015 show, *From the Animals' Perspective*, was, the adults agreed, the most cogent script yet, a gripping rumination on empathy. After extended curtain calls, we made a string of construction paper flags—the Banner of Gratitude, we called it. Everyone got a triangle to decorate or dedicate. At the dinner table, we went around one by one, naming the one person we were most thankful to have met that year: a new baseball coach; Lambchop, a poodle mutt that Liz had brought home for the kids; a researcher doing a clinical trial in Arizona.

After dinner, while the kids cleared the table and Andy and Edward attacked the dishes, Liz slipped away to bed. She'd held up as long as she could. I followed behind, getting in next to her. I wasn't afraid; I'd done this before.

We knew it wouldn't be much longer. Her abdomen had been drained twice in the last week, both times removing more than ten liters of fluid called ascites. Greenie had the same procedure in his final month.

We pretended we were going to watch Viola Davis manhandle the Philly police department in *How to Get Away with Murder*, but after a few minutes Liz snapped off the TV.

"I want to see next year's play," she said.

"I know."

She told me she couldn't take it anymore. She was too tired and the pain was too much. She said she wanted to die at home. "Right here," she said, "in this bed."

"Then you will," I said.

I cried and kissed her hand, which was the only part of her that did not hurt. We stayed in that moment for a long time, crying and looking at each other, until I said out loud for the first time, "I will really miss you." I told her that I didn't know, back when we first danced to Super Booty, that she would become so much more to me than Edward's friend's wife. I told her how much I had wanted to know her and that the conversations we'd been having over the last year or two were the most profound and intimate of my life. I told her she was special, interesting, and specific. I told her she was irreplaceable. She told me I had helped, that I had done "a really good job" being her friend. She said, "Thank you, thank you, Kelly." I said, "I'm so happy I got to really know you," and promised to keep her alive to her children, to tell them everything I knew about her as many times as they wanted, until I was too old to talk or make sense. Before I left, both of us sobbing, I held her cheeks and kissed her on the lips three times.

Two weeks later, on December 12, right there in her bed, she died.

• • •

Not long after, I went to a fundraiser in San Francisco to learn about a nonprofit called Camp Kesem for kids whose parents have, or had, cancer. Edward was back east for work, so I had to go solo.

The event was in an obscenely posh club called The Battery. A glass elevator carried guests to the penthouse where a dashing bartender with a beefy mustache greeted us with the specialty cocktail, which he assured us was made with their best tequila. Teenage campers, conspicuous in their youth and sincerity, circulated among hundreds of guests, thanking us for coming. Don Julio warmed my innards. I allowed my glass to be refilled sooner than perhaps was wise.

The program started with a video set to a well-chosen anthem and closed with a plea for each of us to contribute "in our own unique way." I happened to be sitting next to the camp's director, a persuasive and highly educated woman, for-merly with Bain Consulting, and before I could stop myself, I suggested my contribution might be to volunteer at one of their campsites over the summer. Maybe I could lead journaling projects for the kids or write something to help the home office represent the camp experience to the larger world. She handed me her iPhone and asked me to enter my information into her contacts.

Four months later, long after the night's magic had worn off, I drove three hours east to Grizzly Flats, California, where eighty-five kids and fifty-one counselors were spending five nights together in the cabins of Leoni Meadows.

"Tell me again," Edward said when I called him from the car, "why didn't you just donate like everyone else?"

"Blame the Don Julio," I said, though we both knew it was about Liz, and finding a way to stay close to her.

My first morning, in the dining hall over coffee crystals and a creamer product I hope never crosses my lips again, I sat at the far end of a long table with a counselor, a giant college rugby player whose nickname was Tiny. "This is a place where people *get it*," he said, cutting through a stack of four pancakes with the side of his fork. "It's like a giant empathy pit. For one, these kids know how unpredictable feelings can be. They're laughing one minute and bawling the next and then a second later, they're running off to a Silly String station." Tiny tipped his chin toward a couple of kids who were drawing on each other's forearms with chubby colored markers. "Or tattooing each other. There's no expectation of some linear progression from agony to okayness. It goes in circles. It's sloppy."

A brown-eyed counselor with a high ponytail put her hand on Tiny's shoulder and threw a leg over the bench to sit down. "Kelly, this is Cookie," Tiny said. "She's in charge this week."

"Hi there," I said as she shook my hand.

"Cookie graduates in June," Tiny said with pride. "Then she's going to be the secretary of education."

"That's the plan," Cookie replied.

"We were just talking about how crazy grown-up the kids are," Tiny said.

"Yeah," Cookie said, "they're seriously more mature than half the people we go to college with." Tiny laughed. "You should hear the things they tell us. They come in with so much on their minds, and then, over the week, as they get used to not suppressing so much, you really hear it all. . . ."

"That must be hard, knowing how to respond."

"We don't do much of the talking, actually. The kids all jump in."

"They take care of each other," Tiny said.

"And there's never *pity,*" she said, like *pity* was the dirtiest word she knew.

Turned out, when Cookie was nine, her mom died of lung cancer. She taught elementary school and liked tennis. I said I was sorry, but Cookie shook me off.

"That's why I love being with these kids, being a part of this." She looked out across the cafeteria. "Everyone here knows what it's like. You know, when your mom dies, or your dad, it becomes your life. It's all-consuming because everyone is reacting to it. It's driving *everyone's* behavior—your coaches, your teachers, your mailman. It's super isolating. But not here."

"Last night during Cabin Chat," Tiny said, "one of my guys was talking about The Look. He was at his baseball banquet and all the moms kept giving him The Look, like they felt so sorry for him, and all he wanted to be was a normal kid getting his certificate like everyone else."

"Yup," Cookie said. She tapped her watch. "We gotta roll. We're staging a food fight happening at ten a.m. in the side field."

"Kids need to be kids," Tiny explained to me. "Especially these kids."

"Hold on one sec, I want to introduce Kelly to Lucy," Cookie said, putting her hand on my arm while she looked past me, scanning dozens of faces. "There she is. Lucy is a child genius."

I followed Cookie to Lucy, a twelve-year-old with delicate features and ballerina proportions. She wore mascara and had masked a small pimple with a dab of cover-up. We both looked like we might be layered in all the clothes we'd brought—a dense layer of clouds over the valley made it hard to get warm. Before Cookie left us, she told me that Lucy wanted to be a vet.

"Or a pediatrician," Lucy said. More or less the same thing, I thought.

Lucy and I walked outside and sat down on a

log, our feet stretched out before us in grass that was still wet with the night. The entire camp would gather here soon for midmorning cheers.

"So, this is your first time at Kesem," Lucy said, with the posture, diction, and pride of a concierge. "This is my seventh summer."

To loosen her up, I asked a few dumb questions, like "If you were stranded on a desert island what would you bring?"

"A boat?" she said, like I'd asked a trick question. I laughed. "And a solar cellphone and my dad's watch," she added, holding out her wrist. She'd been wearing it, she explained, since she was five, when he died of pancreatic cancer. "They thought it was the flu." By the time he was correctly diagnosed, the disease was unstoppable.

We talked about her father, his long and happy career at Napa Auto Parts, how much he'd loved country music.

"I still miss him. But that's normal," she told me as she reorganized her hair into a fresh ponytail. "There's no one right way to feel bad, to want something you can't have. And there's no one right way to feel better."

"This is *my* dad's watch," I said, pulling up my sleeve to show her Greenie's drugstore Timex. "He died in February." She looped her arm through mine like we hadn't just met, resting her delicate fingers on my forearm. "My friend died too," I blurted out. "Young, like your dad.

93

I've been thinking about her, and her family, a lot since I got here, seeing all these kids."

"It's weird, the reminders. Like, someone will put on sunblock across the room and the smell—my dad was always putting sunblock on me, I burn easily. . . ." She trailed off and then picked up her own thought. "Or pickle smell. My dad loved pickles."

"I almost burst into tears in a meeting last week," I said. "One of the guys at the table was wearing Old Spice and I felt like my dad was standing behind me."

"How about your friend?" Lucy asked. "What reminds you of her?"

"Tom Petty."

Right then, as the first campers headed down the hill for morning cheers, twelve-year-old Lucy, who probably didn't know Tom Petty from Ben Bernanke, ran her nearly weightless hand back and forth across my back and said what I wish everyone would say—not "I'm sorry" but "I know." Is there a broth more restoring than company?

I asked her if, among her friends at home, she is considered the wise one.

"Yeah, I am." She unzipped her jacket as the sun finally hit us.

I asked her if her relationships back at school were more superficial than here at camp.

"Not superficial, just—I don't know—*limited,*"

Lucy said, wowing me with her insight and lack of judgment, while also making me wonder if *limited* was a neutral descriptor she had learned in grief counseling.

"They won't always be," I said. "I'm fifty. Just about everyone's broken at my age. My friend Katie, back when she was about your age, her dad left her mom and her mom just fell apart. Katie knew what day their mortgage was due starting in fifth grade. By high school, she was writing the checks. All that time, what really tore her up was how everyone felt so sorry for her."

"Everybody in my town thinks of me as *that poor girl,*" Lucy said. "I hate it."

"I had another friend, Anne; her first baby was a stillborn." I looked at Lucy to be sure she understood what that meant. She indicated she did by wincing. "For almost a year after it happened, no one asked her for anything. Her husband, her parents, her friends, they all stopped counting on her. She wanted to crawl out of her skin."

"I hate being treated like a little kid," Lucy said. "I don't want everyone to do everything for me."

"I know."

Lucy got to her feet. Counselors were taking their positions in front of the crowd of kids. It was time for morning cheers.

Watching Lucy fall in with the other campers, I

could imagine their nightly Cabin Chats, the slow nod of deep knowing, the *me-too*'s and *totally*'s.

The next day I asked Cookie, "Do you think broken people are better?"

"It's a big price to pay," she said with tears in her eyes. "But yes. I do." She told me about her boyfriend. They'd been together for a few years and were *definitely* getting married. He had life experience to match hers; not the same but equal in its toll. He knew about adults whispering in the living room, drinking or sleeping or crying at odd hours. Cookie said she couldn't imagine being with "a regular person."

I smiled, adoring this charming, broken girl and the way she saw the world. *Regular people,* who needs them?

About a year before she died, my friendship with Liz left the familiar and became singular.

As her body slowed down, she started to share with me what felt like *everything:* how long it had been since she'd had sex, or wanted to; how much she had spent on a pair of heels that she never wore; how much a certain relative was dragging her down; how excruciating bowel movements had become; how if one more person gave her weed, she'd be considered a dealer in the eyes of the law; what kind of second wife she wanted for Andy.

I had earned the intimacy not because I'd done

chemo myself, but because I'd told her about changing my father's diaper in his final days and buttering up his nurses and crying to a stunned and awkward pharmacist. I'd told her how, after he passed, I considered pocketing his dentures and taking them home with me because I loved his smile so much. I'd told her about letting a friend pay for five hundred printed programs at Greenie's memorial because I didn't have the energy to fight him about it. I'd told her that I was sometimes embarrassed by the extent of my grief over Greenie. "He was eighty-four," I'd said. "Who cries this much about a man dying at eighty-four?"

Knowing people takes time, which we all swear we don't have, or some mitigating circumstance like being caught in an elevator, or war. Huddled in the foxhole, Liz and I said it all. We were judgmental and bitchy together—desperate and existential too. Occasionally, we were our highest and bravest selves, working our way through the darkest ideas. I was lucky to know Liz that well, to know anyone that well. You can't be *really* loved if you can't bear to be *really* known.

I promised Liz that after she died, I would remember the full range of her, the striving and self-doubt, the exasperation and remorse and crazy hope, the ways Andy bugged her and how she adored him. What I wish I'd known then, so I could have told her, was that every important conversation I have, for the rest of my life, will have a little bit to do with her, and Cookie and Lucy, all of whom prove that we can be damaged and heavy-hearted but still buoyant and insightful, still essential and useful, just by saying *I know*.

No

You will be impressed when I tell you that I once swore off cheese, in all its forms and flavors, for ten years. These are just some of the things I did not eat during that decade: lasagna, mac and cheese, nachos, cheeseburgers, grilled cheese, Ro-Tel dip, mozzarella sticks, bagels with cream cheese, cheese puffs, Cheese Curls, cheesecake, Cheez-Its, Cheetos. I wish I could say my sacrifice was an ethical stand taken to bring attention to some injustice—say, dairy farmers befouling the waterways with methane-rich manure—but the truth is it was only to cover a lie I told to my mother.

It was 1976, the summer of the U.S. Bicentennial. I remember because my mom, who disapproved of jewelry on children, let me wear pewter clip-on Liberty Bell earrings. My ninth birthday was wrapping up. As I stood in my driveway and waved off the last guest, I began what I now know is called a postmortem. The party was fine, I told myself, but next year, I wanted more of a theme, something to give the event shape.

But what did we have to offer? Tag? Othello? Sewing? Mrs. Mather, my mother's longtime bridge partner, had a pool. *Imagine that*. We could play sharks and minnows and do cannonball contests. After races, games, and trophies, we could drape ourselves around the edges of the pool, sipping fresh-squeezed somethings with decorative fruit slices.

When I presented my vision to my parents that night, with a seriousness that belied the twelve months we had to plan, my mom said something about liability and my dad said he was sure Mrs. Mather would love to host. He won.

But about a month before my birthday, my friend Allison turned ten, and guess what she did? She had a pool party. In her very own pool. For a party gift, her mom handed out towels, with Hawaiian-print fish pockets she sewed on herself.

"We should just cancel my whole birthday," I moped.

"People make the party," my mother said. "Let's do something in the basement, where it's nice and cool."

Our basement? No one would host an event in that smelly dungeon, even after my parents converted it from a cinderblock afterthought to a wood-paneled Fun Room. The low ceiling was finished with foam tiles we'd sometimes pop out with shirt hangers for *no damn reason*. The plaid wall-to-wall was green and a super-charged orange. Seating was limited to a sofa covered in a thick material I'd be hard-pressed to identify, though I can say it was probably best cleaned with Armor All. Décor aside, what would we do? Play office with a box of letterhead my dad brought home from his job at *McCall's*?

For my brothers, there were floor-hockey sticks and plastic pucks and our most recent addition, the behemoth that appeared one Christmas morning: a regulation-size pool table. How my parents got it in the house I don't know, but I wouldn't have been any more dumbfounded to discover bison down there. Beyond the mystery of its transport, the pool table enlarged my sense of the Possible. Maybe this giant toy meant we were now rich. Maybe we'd start collecting statues, or driving foreign cars, or buying real Oreos instead of Hydrox.

"Maybe we could do a pool party with the *pool table*," my mom said.

"What?"

"I was just thinking—"

"Mom—Jesus!"

"Oh, are we praying now?" she said, as she did when someone took the Lord's name in vain. Then she shrugged and went back to paying bills, audibly licking each envelope.

We could, I supposed, bring cushions down from the upstairs sofas and put them on folding chairs and somehow create a circle of seating around the pool table. Maybe make collage posters with my dad's old magazines, play Truth or Dare. Yeah, that could work. For lunch, each girl could order her own hoagie.

"What do you think, Mom?"

"Sounds good." She didn't even look up. "Except the hoagie thing."

She had nothing against hoagies, per se; she ate one a week herself, though slowly, over the course of several days, one quarter at a time, with half a can of Bud Light poured into a glass. Her sticking points were price per unit, hassle factor, and waste. At $5.40 each, ten hoagies would double the party budget. Then there was the headache of special requests, which are to be expected when ordering anything for ten-year-old girls. Finally, and most objectionably: the notion of picked-over, half-eaten food that could not be salvaged.

She countered with one large cheese pizza and a chocolate sheet cake. This from a woman who had purchased *a pool table* for her sons.

"Mooom! Why can't everyone get their own hoagie?"

"Kelly, those girls can't finish *half* a hoagie. They'll love pizza."

"I won't!" I said.

"Why?"

"Because—I hate cheese."

"No one hates cheese, Kelly."

"I do!"

"Since when?"

"Since forever."

"You had a cheeseburger on Saturday, you had macaroni and cheese last—"

"No I didn't. I didn't eat them."

"Oh, for God's sake, you most certainly did. It's pizza or nothing."

I growled like a terrier. There were no words. I hated her that much.

On the day of the party, which was lackluster until the moment the pizza came, I abstained conspicuously, putting a small pile of potato chips in the center of my paper plate, hoping to God someone would ask me about it so I could articulate my plight. (No one did.) Later, when my mom was cleaning up, I took a leftover piece of pizza and removed the cheese, now congealed into a rubbery sheet, with the very tips of my fingers like it was a dead bird, and dropped it into the sink.

"Suit yourself," she said as she pushed the cheese down the disposal. She did not offer to boil me a hot dog. Or make me a PB&J.

It was a tiresome decade, picking Parmesan off my pasta, ordering plain hamburgers at Burger King, eating only the crust of cheesecakes. I fucking loved cheese. But believe me, it was worth it. She was, as all mothers are, my first *everything*. First refuge, first rival. I was showing her how formidable I could be, meal by meal, year by year, as she was showing me how formidable she could be. She never once played along with my "allergy." If I was waiting for her to apologize for ruining my birthday, I would wait forever.

Recently, while we were visiting her in Philly, Claire asked about the expression *cutting off your nose to spite your face,* which is one of the more gruesome aphorisms to parse for a child.

"Here's a great example," I said. "When I was ten—" My mom leaned in the room. "I'm just telling Claire how I gave up cheese."

"You did what?"

"Cheese. I gave up cheese. Remember?"

She considered. "Did you?"

"The hoagie thing . . . my birthday . . . I didn't eat cheese. . . ." I waited for recollection to wash over her. "You made me get pizza and I said I wouldn't eat it because I hated cheese and you got it anyway, so I didn't eat it and then I never—"

She smiled, amused. "Oh, you." If a girl screams at a tree in a forest until it falls just to make her mother crazy, but her mother goes about her business unfazed, did the tree really fall? "That does sound like a good example of cutting the nose on your face, or whatever."

Unlike my mother, sometimes I am seized by an overpowering (and pathetic) need to make my children like me. This feeling is quite a surprise

104

to me. I thought I had more personal conviction than to chase approval ratings, and from such fickle customers. But it keeps happening.

One rainy weekend a few years back, I was trying to jack up my popularity when I found myself in one of those mall islands—you know, the shops without walls that float in the current of foot traffic and before you know it, you're in it?

My daughters had slowed to a stop, mesmerized by a dozen hairstyling instruments positioned in a row of stainless-steel holsters. I looked my typical terrible—mascara from the night before bending my eyelashes in weird ways, a shirt most people would press. A wave of self-consciousness splashed up against me as the goddess who governed the island rotated on her spikes and shone her glorious countenance upon us. She was definitely one of those women who showered every day.

No need to be ashamed, Old Lady, her gaze seemed to say. *It's not you I'm after.* Her Persian Princess eyes landed on Georgia, whose hair was thrown up into a spiky bun. *Come . . . try . . .* she beckoned, waving my daughter toward a throne of white pleather.

Here was the getaway moment. This is when the shrewd consumer drops her gaze and scurries her charges along. But as my chance to step away from the light passed, I said a series of things that were not no, things like "Yeah, we have a minute" and "Sure, I guess she can sit" and "You know, we *did* buy a cheap drugstore flatiron and we *were* disappointed."

With each stroke of the miraculous wand, my daughter's mound of hair became the stunning locks of shampoo commercials—good shampoo like Pantene Smooth and Sleek.

The goddess had more questions.

"Doesn't this look easy?" *Yes*.

"Can you see how the ceramic protects the ends?" *Amazing*.

In minutes, Claire was in the seat and another transformation had begun.

"Look." She wrapped Claire's fingers around the wand. "Even Little Sister can do it." *Well, I'll be damned.*

While the girls marveled at their makeovers, a call was made to a man in faraway ManagerLand to ask for a *very special price* for *two young women* to have this product, and the *critical* argan oil that came with it for a *small additional fee*. During their hushed conversation, the girls glanced at me anxiously like finalists in a beauty pageant awaiting word from the judges. I was already in. It's fun to say yes. Everyone loves you when you say yes. Was there a price too high to make my children like me, embrace me, smile all afternoon and for the rest of their lives? Four minutes later, we rode down the escalator, the girls giddy and victorious while I followed behind, $200 lighter. A classic chump.

#nevernotonce did my mother indulge me in the name of a hug. She didn't even like hugs. Mary Corrigan knew a cheap yes was a cigarette buzz, passing in minutes, leaving you sour-stomached and polluted, somewhere you don't want to be, doing something you don't want to do, with no one but y-o-u to blame.

Back in my twenties, over beers in a parking lot after watching a Notre Dame lacrosse game, one of my cousins asked me if my parents were getting a divorce.

"What?" I said.

My cousin's oh-come-on expression pissed me off and spooked me at the same time.

"They're never together," he said. "I see your dad all the time and your mom is never with him."

"Oh, *that*." I was too inexperienced with relationships to understand or defend their way of being married but not too naïve to have noticed that there *was* something unusual about the way my parents operated. At some point, before my memory, my mom had simply stopped doing things she didn't want to do, appearances be damned: baking, driving at night, doing laundry, and—after a brief stretch in the early sixties, when she was presumably so besotted she'd have gone with Greenie anywhere—escorting her husband to every dumb place he went. My dad would say he was going to a barbecue or a club social and she'd say, "I think I'll take a pass" or "How 'bout I catch you on the flip side?" Her casual responses made it clear: skipping an outing, even one that other wives wouldn't, was "no big whup."

Still, even on the worst days of my childhood, my parents' union felt shatterproof.

"Even when they do go somewhere together," my cousin continued, "they don't drive in the same car." Again, this was technically accurate. "Not even to *church*," he said, like that was too weird for words. Had my cousin asked my mother directly, she would have said this was the only rational response to the cat-herding that played out in our kitchen every Sunday morning of my childhood.

My mother, generally dressed in black pull-on pants and a cropped boiled-wool jacket with shiny brass buttons, would get up from the table first, collecting the dishes closest to her.

"Mom! I'm still eating!" I'd protest.

"You won't starve," she'd say, sliding the last of my English muffin into the sink.

"How many points did Dr. J have?" Booker would ask my dad, who was bogarting the sports page.

"Twenty-eight!"

"George—" my mom would say, shutting off the water, eyeing the clock.

My dad would signal some small measure of compliance, like pushing back from the table, while holding tight to the paper. "And eight rebounds—"

"George, mass starts in six minutes!" She may have been raised by a German who snapped into action but she married an Irishman who rolled.

"I'm on it, Mare!" He'd push back from the table another inch or two, as if he cared about punctuality. "Mo Cheeks put up eighteen," he'd whisper to my brothers.

"What time are the Flyers on tonight?" GT would ask.

"George, for Pete's sake!"

"You heard your mother, boys. Let's go."

"Honestly, must we go through this *every single week?*" she would say as she rolled Cover Girl Coral Reef across her lips. "Leaving in one minute!" she'd call up the stairs, as if we were actually that close to passing inspection and getting in the car. Between this moment and that, there could easily be an outfit violation, a fight over chewing gum, or a phone call from any one of my father's brothers, all while my mother stood by the door in her wool coat, purse on her arm, eyebrows high with incredulity. On any Sunday morning at 168 Wooded Lane from 1969 to 1980, you could find four people pressing one woman's every button. Until that woman said *No. No more. I'll see you there.*

Taking two cars to church led to taking two cars to the pool, which led to taking two cars to sporting events, which meant my mother could slip away the moment the game had become predictable, leaving my dad to linger unencumbered, which led to going to fewer games entirely.

Ice hockey, played at ungodly hours in dumpy locales where rent is cheap and seating is hard, asks a lot of its fans. And for what? Rather than tough it out and hope for a Golden Mommy badge at the annual awards dinner, my mother would "take a smart pill" and bow out. As for lacrosse, she was happy to stop by my brothers' home games, but away games? Under the threat of spring showers? No chance. Greenie not only rearranged his sales calls so that he could be settled in the stands by four p.m. but, thanks to a sprawling network of fellow enthusiasts and an uncanny nose for any game in the area, he was as apt to pop by any decent match-up within twenty miles. If that set him up for a few beers after at the local pub, followed by a quick burger, so be it. One fewer mouth to feed for my mother.

On Saturday mornings, Greenie played tennis, squash, or golf. My mother was not interested in breaking a sweat, but if a game could be played at her kitchen table while she sipped her Sanka in her baby-blue terrycloth bathrobe and white slippers that made her feet look like bunnies, she was all in. She still does the daily jumble, the crossword, and Sudoku. In terms of activities she would put on a bra and leave the house for, there was only bridge, which she played expertly several times a week.

None of this is to suggest she wasn't a devoted sports fan. (She could have subbed in for Dick Enberg on an hour's notice, such was the depth of her expertise.) Nor is it to imply that my mother didn't love Greenie and his company. (She did, completely.) She just didn't abide by the scripture that said love meant shared hobbies, matching personalities, and standing on muddy sidelines listening to amped-up parents relive man-down plays while you wish you were home icing your lower back and having some vodka. She certainly didn't believe in making public appearances to satisfy a mouthy nephew who doubted whether her marriage was intact.

"*Chacun à son gout*," she liked to say in an exaggerated French accent. *To each his own.* If her husband was an extrovert who mainlined interaction, and she an introvert who found the whole thing exhausting—well then, she would set him free to socialize "to his heart's content." My mother had her own mind and she used it.

She didn't demand her way, but she didn't pretend to be without preference, either. She had no desire to curb another's activities. If my brothers and I wanted to go to Minella's Diner for eggs and pancakes and she couldn't think of anything worse, she'd wave us goodbye from the kitchen table, where she'd enjoy her English muffin in front of her kerosene heater while she listened to her Perry Como cassette. *A Party for One,* she called it.

Very few people I've known are able to set themselves free the way my mother has. Liberated by the simple act of saying no—which I submit is impressive for any woman, and downright radical for one raised in the Nice'n Easy generation—my mom had always been able to find outs where others could not. Looking back, I think it came down to her impressive willingness to be disliked and her utterly unromantic position that people should take serious—if not total—responsibility for their own happiness. This extended to all corners of her life, including her birthdays. My mother not only made lists of gift ideas but also posted them on the family bulletin board and attached coupons. She knew what would make her day a good one. To hide the answer was to burden us with a silly guessing game we would surely lose. (In my utopian view, drafting a shortlist of affordable trinkets for the girls to buy me would be to drain all meaning from the gift. Shouldn't they *just know?*)

As she neared her seventieth birthday, my brothers and I decided to pool resources and get her a more substantial present than we could afford individually. We tried to loop in Greenie, but he had already decided on a diamond elephant brooch, a nod to her deeply felt Republicanism, disregarding years of experience that told him that strictly ornamental gifts would be returned for cash.

"So, Mom, anything big you've been wanting?" I asked on a visit several months before her birthday. Though my brothers and I would cough up whatever it cost, I suspected that whatever she might have in mind would be on a par with birthdays past; bath salts or a wrinkle cream or possibly something mysterious but affordable like 2001's request for a paraffin wax bath (for "softer, more youthful hands").

"I know *exactly* what I want from you kids." She'd loaded this gun a month ago.

"Really?" I went from eager-to-please to anxious. What if she was thinking a trip to Hawaii? A new Oldsmobile? Had my magnanimous phrasing put us all in a corner?

"Absolutely," she said. "If there is *any problem* that you or your brothers have that I can help with, I would like to know about it."

I held out my arms so she could see the raised hairs. "God, Mom," I said. "You're killing me here."

She put her finger up to indicate that she was not quite finished. "And if there's any problem that you or your brothers have that there is *nothing whatsoever* that I can do to change, I would like to *not* know about it."

I laughed like she was kidding.

"Listen, Kelly, I've been a mother since 1964. And I would like to stop worrying and get some sleep."

Sleep. That's what she wanted. Sleep, which she could not possibly have if we continued to tell her every troubling detail of our lives, our children's lives. No to stories of heartache, of ornery teachers and short-tempered coaches, of stretches of unshakable sadness. No to insinuations about marriage trouble, lost investments, career setbacks. No to detailed reports of lower back pain, erratic sleeping, looming hip surgery.

She had tracked the three of us for forty-five years, internalizing every broken bone and paper cut, every missed promotion, separation, and lost election, every invitation that didn't come or that was revoked. She had fixed or tried to fix every fixable thing. *Now,* if you pleased, *no more.*

I understood. I'd tried to pull back from the drama Georgia and Claire brought home, strung out by the sound of their tears, the sight of them balled up in bed. I'd stay downstairs for a minute or two, manically cleaning the counters, but I always went up, with a glass of ice water or a bowl of apples cored and cut just the way they like them. And I'd only been mothering for ten years. How many Guatemalan worry dolls might

I have rubbed to pieces after twenty-nine more?

About four days after my mother asked me to stop troubling her with problems she could not reasonably hope to fix, I mentioned that Claire had cried herself to sleep the night before.

"Oh wait, sorry," I caught myself. "Happy birthday."

"Thank you," she said firmly.

The next morning, I woke up to a text from her: *How's my Claire Bear?*

Sexually, professionally, personally, saying no takes balls. One friend told me her one big take-away from three years and $11,000 of therapy was *Learn to say no. And when you do, don't complain and don't explain. Every excuse you make is like an invitation to ask you again in a different way.*

You might have thought, raised as I was by a no pro, that I'd be a real ass-kicker, like the much-hazed pledge who becomes a power-drunk master. Ha.

I couldn't say no to a recent haircut that made me look like a businessman from the seventies, or to a nearly abusive masseuse who asked, *Does this feel good?,* or to a coy babysitter who asked if she could have a friend or two over after the kids went to bed and then left joints on the deck. I like to project breezy and happy-go-lucky; I pooh-pooh high-maintenance types and their excessive instructions: *Layered around the face and bangs to my eyebrows, and remember, my hair gets a lot shorter as it dries. Light pressure along the spine but deep around the shoulders. No dessert for the kids, they both need baths, and please run the dishwasher.* Who takes her haircut, a massage, one evening of her life that seriously? But in my devotion to the casual ideal, I have accidentally created a false choice between being easy to do business with and having any opinion at all. It must be possible to say no nicely and still be loved.

What else should I have said no to?

Bringing forgotten lunches to school. Back-to-back sleepovers. Snapchat.

No to talking back, bad language, shouting. No to *Bridesmaids* and *Step Brothers*.

No to Jane Doe when she looked across the playground and said, *Don't you think that kid is bad news?*

No to John Doe when he gestured toward two guys cleaning our cars and said, *These people are not exactly known for their work ethic, know what I mean?*

No to orthodontia before middle school.

No to AppleCare and rental car insurance upgrades.

No to traveling over Thanksgiving, the T.J.Maxx credit card, the aspirational gym membership.

No to TV in the bedroom.

No to "pre-parties."

No to unpaid work.

No to the third season of *The Bachelorette*.

Little noes prepare us for the big noes that define the major movements of our lives. The job we shouldn't take, the relationship we must leave, the deal that seems shady. No, finally, to another drink, no to abuse, no to getting back together again. No to extreme life-saving measures.

When we were children, no came so easily to the lips. Wearing a coat? Turning off the TV? Leaving your sister alone? No chance. But then we became civilized. We aged into self-consciousness. Saying no started to feel rude or insubordinate, mean or lazy, withholding or dangerous. There's hardly a positive intention associated with no.

Except self-preservation.

I always wanted four kids; "Four by forty" was the way I put it when the subject of family first surfaced with Edward. Greenie was from six, my mom from four. Four is enough for a dance party, a touch football team, a human pyramid. And kids from big families are funny—something about having to earn attention or live without it. Gimme a litter of possums over a couple precious koalas any day. Trouble was, by the time I married my Arkansas prince, I was thirty-two. With less than ten years to make good on my slogan, I dragged Edward straight from the honeymoon to the breeding shed.

Georgia, in one of the great blessings of my life, came easily; one try. Claire took a bit more time but not so much that the plan was spoiled. I had a little more than four years to come up with two more. A few months after Claire was born, I dried out my jugs, my periods returned and we started tracking my ovulation again. Three months passed, then six, then ten—no luck. Just after Claire turned one, I discovered that nasty tumor in my breast, and the chemo that followed suspended my fertility, as chemo sometimes does. In terms of remission, this was good news. My cancer liked estrogen; it used it to multiply. Everyone was happy but me. "Four by forty" was slipping to "Four by forty-three," which had neither a ring to it nor particularly strong odds.

Then, about a year later, when my periods surprised us all by returning, it was highly recommended that I take medication to *suppress ovarian function*. I hadn't quite seen this coming. Edward and my oncologist were insistent and even though I can be bold, I was not deaf to the argument that this was a time for caution. I acquiesced, but still harbored hope for more kids. Maybe after a year, I told myself, when everyone sees how healthy I am. It became a moot point when, at thirty-eight, one of my ovaries developed a troubling growth and to keep me safe from the devastation that is ovarian cancer, a surgeon named Mindy signed me up for an oophorectomy, a Suessian-sounding operation during which my ovaries were snipped from my fallopian tubes, pulled through tiny slits in my lower belly, and discarded in a bio-waste bag, along with any hope of another pregnancy. Or two.

Though I cried a lot during that time, I also knew that one need not carry a baby to have a baby. I had seen MH become a mother through adoption, twice. I had watched my friend Nancy find a surrogate to grow her family. It went so well she did it again. (She now has five kids.) I called a few services to learn more. The surrogate route turned out to be beyond us financially, but once Google announced me to the family planning community, Internet cookies bombarded me with banner ads featuring photos of happy families, exciting testimonials, and bold promises like *seamless* and *complete*. Adoption, domestic and international; egg and embryo donors. There were pages of links to explore. I talked to counselors over the phone. I had a preliminary conversation with my sister-in-law, who said she would actually consider carrying a child for us. Options were mounting. I created a spreadsheet in Excel to capture costs, risks, and legalities. At night, as I did my final check on the girls, I'd whisper into their ears, *I'm gonna get you a little sister or brother, just you wait.*

If we could *seamlessly complete* our family, why wouldn't we?

A great believer in timing, I waited for the ideal moment to sit down with Edward and share My Vision.

Two months later, on a five-hour flight to the East Coast, with the girls plugged into *Finding Nemo,* I saw my opening. I pulled my spreadsheet out of my carry-on. Whatever anxieties or objections he might have, I was prepared to address them. He would be convinced. Short of that, he loved me—he would want me to have what I wanted.

I eased into my pitch: We had much to celebrate, I said. Claire was potty trained, Georgia had a wiggly tooth, everyone was finally sleeping through the night. Edward closed his book, holding his page with his finger. He could sense where this was headed. I kept going: I was healthy again, I said, no bone pain, no mouth sores. It was all so faint now, the outlines of that very hard time barely visible in the bright light of where we were headed.

Edward agreed. He peeked at his page number and slid his book into the seat pocket in front of him. I took his hand.

"And I'm on a good run with work," he said, "so

I think we can take a good trip this summer. . . ."

"Definitely. But I've also been exploring some other possibilities."

"For what?"

"For more kids."

His eyes narrowed in a way I didn't like. "O-kay," he said.

I lowered his tray table and set down the spreadsheet. "All right, here are all our options." He didn't cut me off but his back was stiff.

I went through my list—egg donor, surrogate, adoption. I could tell by the knit of his eyebrows that the dominant emotion rising in him was not agreement or even curiosity but pity, for me, whose dearest wish he would not indulge.

"Just listen," I said, pushing back against the message his face was sending. "This is totally workable. People do it all the time. We haven't had to think like this, but it's all here, all the options, and all the pros and cons, and the contacts in each place—"

He sighed.

"What?" I said.

"I'm happy, Kelly." His tone was gentle, but unequivocal. "My wife is back to full strength. My kids are good. I can afford my life. I have no battles to wage. And I don't want a new one." The sounds of the flight hummed in my ears. I couldn't look at him. For the first time in our marriage, we were looking at a big decision and seeing something different. I bit my lip and looked at my hands in my lap. I was mad and separate and undone. There was kindness in his voice when he spoke again. "I just want to enjoy what we have. I want to be the family we are."

Though I cried, I didn't fight him. How could I? Edward had never once cursed my disease for upending *his* life, for the angst it must have caused him. In fact, his stiff-upper-lip act had been so convincing, I hadn't appreciated that he, too, was recovering. And though I barely noticed him noticing, he had followed along as MH braved five years of crippling fertility treatments and harrowing adoption proceedings. "I'm sorry, Kelly. I can't."

I nodded, wiped under my eyes. There was nothing more to be said on the matter. There's no acquiescing on some things; they're too defining, too consequential.

He held my hand for the next hour while I began dismantling a collage of vivid and detailed images I had collated over the years; reshuffling bedrooms to accommodate number three, someone new growing into the tiny Levi's Georgia used to love, becoming that cool, relaxed parent I'd always imagined being thanks to the extra years of experience.

Rather than trying to *make me happy,* as cheap pop songs and misguided greeting cards suggest is the promise of true love, Edward was doing the one thing that would keep us together: taking care of himself. As with my parents, sometimes the art of relationship is declaring your limits, protecting your boundaries, saying no.

Thanks to Edward and my mother, whose nonchalant self-possession I've fallen a little bit in love with as of late, I've not only managed to decline an invitation to join a project, attend an event, and donate to several causes I don't care that much about, but I've come to feel downright uneasy with people who can't say no. What if they yes you to death and then secretly hate you for it? If they never say no, how can you trust their yes? Besides, no makes room for yes, and who doesn't want more room for that?

Yes

Here's a running list of things I'll always say yes to:

Backgammon, rummy 500, a dice game
    called pig
Cracked pepper, grated Parmesan, extra
    guac
Corzo tequila, licorice mint tea, seltzer
Salted caramel, salted rim, salty jokes
More sleep, more volume, more help
Books with a deckle edge
A second opinion
The heated-seat option
A B. J. Novak short story, a Richard
    Thompson performance
Feedback
Communion
My mom
Dinner at Beth Barrett's house
A swim in the lake, a train ride, square
    dances, wig parties, charades
A second chance, but maybe not a third
An incoming call from Tracy Tuttle,
    Cousin Kath, Liz's Andy
Hiring a professional nitpicker

Sex with my husband (because what if he dies in his sleep?)

Notting Hill, Michael Clayton, Willy Wonka & the Chocolate Factory (the original one)

A lecture

A kid—even the one who is several inches taller than me—wanting to sleep with us

Tylenol PM

Spellcheck, Spanx, scarves, sleeping in

A Philly cheesesteak with hots and sweets

Breath mints

I Was Wrong

Start with this: our dog, Hershey, often takes me over my personal limit. She's had minimal training, a project that was squarely on me, so everything Hershey-related is my fault, which is precisely why her bad behavior has the power to wreck me. It takes a lot of discipline to create discipline and discipline is not something I was born with. I married discipline.

A person less lame than I would teach a dog to keep her snout out of women's crotches, for instance. Googling it has yielded nothing, so when a woman visits our house, she must face this terrible consequence: everyone will wonder what scent the famously sensitive dog nose is picking up. Does Hershey know she is postcoital or infected with yeast or just a woman who hides kibbles in her panties? I have no idea how to stop this and anyway, according to Edward, it's "not worth learning how to retrain Hershey" if "the primary presence" isn't going to "monitor and correct the behavior." Apparently, it's "all about consistency" with dogs. "Like kids," Edward sometimes adds when he is feeling like our marriage is on an extra-strong footing.

Apart from the crotch-sniffing, Hershey's big sin is drinking from toilets, which confounds me as it is demonstrably more difficult than drinking fresh water from the dog bowl I fill for her each morning and set down next to the patch of sun she likes to rest in. That said, lapping up toilet water would not be a problem if Hershey could get her fill without making such a mess. Oh, and also because the toilets in our house are not always empty. Before you judge, let me point out that I came into environmental consciousness in San Francisco, where a lot of people don't flush the toilets every time they tinkle—more like every other time. This saves a lot of water. In the privacy of your own home, on the second floor, I think you can leave a little toilet paper and pee in your bowl. (I also think it's okay to share toothbrushes among family members. I have been told by friends that this is a divisive position to take, but there it is.)

Anyway: sometimes, a child in our home will do *more* than pee in a toilet. In fact, this probably happens once a day for each of them. Most of the time, that child will flush away the evidence of their healthy digestive system. But sometimes—more often than I can handle, frankly—that child will forget to flush.

Guess what a lot of dogs like to eat?

That's right.

So many dogs like to eat it, in fact, there's a name for it. Coprophagia. (From the Internet: "Some veterinary nutritionists have suggested that dogs eat stool to replenish enzymes so that they are better prepared to digest their food. A lack of vitamin B is often said to be a cause of coprophagia.") Hershey, we can deduce, is fully prepared to digest her food and retains dizzying levels of vitamin B.

One morning on my nine a.m. sweep through the second floor—turning off lights, hanging up towels, closing all the dresser drawers my children and husband leave hanging open like so many tongues sticking out at me—I entered the bathroom my daughters share and there, *on the floor,* was the most awful sight one can see in her own home: solid human waste.

"Mother of Jesus Christ Almighty!"

After more blasphemy and outrage, I covered the ordure in many layers of toilet paper and quickly transferred it from tile to toilet. There followed a few awful moments, moments during which one could only ask: *How has my life come to this?*

When my daughters returned from school that afternoon, I held a meeting to convey the gravity of the morning's event. There ensued a solemn discussion about flushing, and more broadly, about me and my role here on Earth, i.e., the things I am more than willing to do as a mother and the few tasks that no one should *ever* have to do.

Georgia bravely said, "I thought I flushed but I

must not have held down the handle-thingy long enough."

"You have to *check*," I said. "Every time. This must never happen again. Do you understand? *Nev-ver.* Say it with me."

"Yes. Mom, I get it."

Fast-forward two weeks to a gray Saturday morning in January.

We were downstairs, the girls enjoying granola with yogurt, myself a cup of strong coffee, Edward his bacon, when I heard a curious splash followed by the jingle of dog tags. Then: more splashing. And I knew. *It's happening.*

"No, no, no!" I flew up the stairs to find Hershey scampering away, back rounded, tail tucked. "I can't fucking deal!"

I still have wrinkles in my forehead that were made that day, standing in the doorway of the bathroom, the one with the darling West Elm shower curtain I'd just hooked onto the rings the night before. I gasped then shifted into a kind of rhythmic, minor-key wailing, like an angry orgasm.

Edward called up the stairs in alarm. "What is it?"

"Auhhhhhh!" I could not yet find words.

The girls and Edward bunched up behind me, looking over my shoulders, beholding the dark matter spread across the lavender tiles.

"It's not mine!" Georgia said, knowing her

prior conviction would make her the prime suspect.

"God fucking *dammit!*" I hollered. "We just talked about this!" That whole big speech I gave, for what?

"I swear, Mom, it's not mine!"

"Oh, for chrissake, we're going to argue about whose shit it was?"

"I *swear*. I remember flushing," Georgia said.

"You didn't. Flush. Hard. Enough!" I punctuated each syllable by smashing the side of my fist into my palm.

"I swear to God," she said. "I didn't do it!"

"Do you think Hershey did it? Do you think she sat herself up on the toilet and—"

"I don't know but I swear on a Bible! I always flush now! You can install video cameras in every bathroom!"

"All right," Edward said, "now we're getting ridiculous."

Oh, fuck you too, Mr. Voice of Reason.

Claire, eager to end the brawl, said, "I'll clean it up."

"Absolutely not!" I roared. Eyes darted between the girls as they backed away from me like I was a bat caught in a house, whipping around in circles. "Georgia will clean it up. Because"—I just barely heard the next string of words for what they were—"in this family, everyone cleans their own goddamn shit off the fucking floor!"

Edward looked at me like I was a transient shouting madnesses on the corner. Georgia went to the kitchen for paper towels, Claire wept quietly, and I left to "walk the fucking dog!," clipping on her leash too fast, yanking her as I stormed up the driveway. My throat throbbed from the yelling. It took a mile to regulate my breathing.

What is wrong with me? I celebrate my spunky daughters on Instagram, but privately smash their spirits to bits over a trivial mistake like not jiggling the handle on an old toilet it might be time to replace?

What have I done? Let's see:

1. I had perfectly modeled all the things I have been railing against for years—accusing, overreacting, "spazzing." If I was hoping either of my children would stop coming unglued over, say, shoes that don't fit or "someone" eating all their Halloween candy, uh, well, maybe not.

2. I had disgraced myself in front of my husband and co-parent, perhaps losing any shred of un-get-back-able respect, perhaps making it impossible for him to ever say with any conviction, "Kelly? Oh, Kelly is *a great mom*." Not even as part of an anniversary card or a birthday toast.

3. Did I just tempt the gods to send me a real problem?

When I returned, Claire was sniffling in my bed, scarred, no doubt, by my rage (more offensive than its inspiration), to say nothing of how deeply unsettling it can be to clean up human shit. I had work to do.

This would require a near-perfect apology. According to my mother, the cornerstone of a proper apology is taking responsibility, and the capstone is naming the transgression. Contrition must be felt *and* conveyed. Finally, apologies are better served plain, hold the rationalizations. In other words, *I'm sorry* should be followed by a pause or period, not by *but* and never by *you*.

Trouble is, by the time you're in kindergarten, *I'm sorry* has been delivered so many times in so many tones, with so many intentions, followed by so much defensive blathering, it could mean anything from *I wish I hadn't started this* to *I want this to end* to *Jeez Louise, all right already, what are you getting so upset about?* That's why I prefer *I was wrong*. It's harder to say. It's singular in meaning. And it reeks of humility.

"Oh, Claire." I leaned in to kiss her, eager for relief. "I was wrong."

"You scared me." She shrank back from me.

"I know. I just—Georgia and I just talked about this whole—"

"Mommy, it was mine."

Could I be more of a mutant?

"Oh, God." I stood at Claire's bedside, only a dozen steps away from where Georgia stewed in her room. Hands on hips, eyes closed, I exhaled again and turned toward the door. Hershey followed me across the hall.

"Hi, G," I said. Her arms were crossed, her expression ice. She knew she had me. Maybe she expected to see me come in on my knees. "So," I said, "I was wrong. I thought Claire's poop was your poop. And even if it had been yours, the way I acted was awful. But—"

"But—?" she said, winding up.

"Nothing. Nothing. I was wrong."

Watch the news for a week and you'll see a dozen stories of people owning their mistakes. During a postgame interview, a white NBA player characterized the Golden State Warriors as "quick little monkeys." The next day, he issued a statement saying he chose the wrong words. A security firm that had been running training in a large arena apologized profusely for accidentally leaving behind a fake pipe bomb that scared the venue personnel who found it. The Canadian prime minister addressed the descendants of a group of immigrants, saying Canada was wrong

133

for turning away their parents and grandparents at the border *in 1914.* A man who had robbed a bank to get his family out of debt apologized, after spending five years in prison, to the bank customers he terrified that day.

So, what am *I* waiting for? Edward suggests I begin with him. Okay:

> Edward Lichty, fine man and husband: about that morning we moved from San Francisco to Berkeley, seventeen years ago . . . While you went to get coffees (which was very thoughtful), I threw out your T-shirts. I shouldn't have done it, but before I could stop myself, I had rolled that dark green Hefty bag into the dumpster. I was wrong. Then I made up that whole thing about seeing the drifter. . . . That was wrong, too.

(Please note that I did not tack on something true like, *But let's face it, hon, those T-shirts were tacky,* because equivocating is for beginners.)

> I'm also sorry that I second-guess your work choices. It must be maddening to tell me about an office conflict and have me take the opposing point of view. I think I do it out of a need for lively engagement, or to hit you with a bit of what the girls

give me, or to prove that I'm smart too, but whatever the reason, it's wrong and I will really try to stop doing it.

And:

> You know how I quietly slip out of the house for a walk while you fight with our insurance over duplicate bills or scour the fine print of every contract we enter into as a couple? It's not right that I leave all the brain-frying work to you— especially since I don't even do the easy stuff, like grocery shopping, until one of the girls' friends opens the fridge and says something thing like *Where do you keep your food?* and then *What do you eat the hummus with?*

But, even as I own up to my wrongs, I wonder if it's ill-advised to call attention to the lesser parts of myself. What if the truth about my character is not that great and this is how word gets out? Not to mention: once I say out loud that I was wrong to toss or undermine or shirk, I can't keep tossing, undermining, or shirking. Being a permanently better partner than I have been seems unlikely and a hair ambitious. It's a daunting combination: exposing our crappiest selves and creating expectations of personal change.

• • •

Greenie's mom was an enormously capable woman who raised six kids on not much more than a sack of greening potatoes. Growing up we saw her three or four times a year. Since I was one of twenty-odd grandchildren streaming in and out of her front door, many of whom lived nearby and knew her better, nothing special was expected of me. I'd say a quick hello and answer one or two questions about my favorite class at school or how tall I'd gotten before she was called away by another relative. To me, Cleta was the short old lady with little gray teeth who was my grandmother. For her children, she was gravity itself.

She had been widowed for a good decade before she felt truly ancient, and even then, in her mideighties, she held on for another two years in a tiny apartment in Baltimore, aided by a full-time nurse named Betty. At the time, I was in my early twenties and also living in Baltimore, working for United Way, a career choice that made me feel like "a good person" who was "changing the world." (It's possible I was an insufferable millennial before there were insufferable millennials.)

In my zeal for self-actualization, I tore through *The 7 Habits of Highly Effective People* and then read it again, slowly, with a fat yellow highlighter in hand. When Dr. Covey implored the reader to "begin with the end in mind" and "put first things first," I nodded and took note. In the workbook pages in the back of the book, I completed a ten-point mission statement which I summarized in capital letters: *BE USEFUL.*

Trouble was, I didn't let any of that high-mindedness affect my personal life. Sure, I posted lines from Covey around my room, about paradigm smashing and prioritizing contributions, but my mindshare was devoted to me, me, me and how tomorrow I might be a better me—more fulfilled, newly promoted, thinner, and in love. No amount of self-reflection could get me to point my used Honda Civic toward the cluster of one-bedroom, single-story apartments called the Elkridge Estates seven miles away, where Greenie's mom sat in her recliner, the tips of her sensible navy pumps grazing the floor below, hoping for a visitor between catnaps.

My cousin Lisa, who worked for Catholic Charities (so was also a do-gooder), managed to visit Cleta once or twice *a week,* stopping in for a game of ten-card gin or a chocolate-covered Berger cookie. She floored me once by saying she hoped to live there, in Cleta's apartment, after she died.

In the two years that I lived in Baltimore, I went to see Cleta once.

It was a sunny day and my boss was at a conference about Planned Giving. I wandered around the office in the morning, took a long walk around the Inner Harbor over lunch, and by three, I couldn't sit at my desk any longer. Heading down the stairs, I rationalized that leaving two hours early to spend ten minutes with my grandmother was, loosely speaking, "family leave." From my office garage, the drive to her complex took twelve minutes. I hadn't put the car in Park before thinking: *How long did Lisa hang around?* and *What if Cleta didn't remember to mention it to my dad?* (An Instagram post about me and Granny *hanging hard* on a Tuesday evening, #wisdom #86+awesome would've done the trick but 1992 offered up no easy tools to document kindly deeds or good hair days.)

When I walked in, Cleta was still as a stone, tucked neatly into her armchair, a game of solitaire suspended on a TV tray beside her. The apartment smelled like sausage. I kissed her hello and her whiskers tickled my lip. I took a seat across from her and talked loudly about things she couldn't possibly relate to: my one-year anniversary at work, a keg party that my roommate and I were hosting that weekend, the new point system at Weight Watchers. She played along, nodding and smiling, so relaxed, in fact, she released a long series of staccato farts that brought to mind the sputtering Wheel of Fortune. When I exhausted my news, she chatted about how Aunt Mary came to see her every day and Aunt Peggy brought her that sweet plant on the windowsill and Uncle Dickie was coming by with clam chowder on Saturday. She recited the same tidbits over and over, skipping from one to the next, each retelling as fresh as the first, until it seemed I'd been there long enough.

I was eager to tell my dad about our visit, but to avoid the long-distance charge, I waited to call him until I got to work the next day.

"Went to see Cleta last night," I said, casually, like I might be that kind of person after all.

"Boy, that's great, Lovey!" Greenie said. "I bet that meant the world to her."

I loved Greenie so much, above all others—you'd have thought I'd have gone to see his mother again in short order just to hear the joy in his voice. But months passed, and the next time I got serious about "finding time" for Cleta (as if I was so busy), a year had gone by.

Not that I hadn't thought about it. Every Sunday evening, at my aunt Mary's grab-bag potluck, Lisa would tell a story about bringing deviled eggs or scones to Cleta and I'd quietly recommit myself to go see her. "This week for sure!" I would write in my journal before going to sleep. But come dawn, I'd be thinking about the upcoming Little Feat concert or how I'd lost four pounds in a month or how much money I would have to save in the next year if I really wanted to go to Australia.

Then, it was over. Greenie called one morning in January when I was at work. "I just got off the phone with your aunt Peggy," he said. "Your grandmother died this morning."

"Aw, God, Dad. I'm so—"

"You should have gone to visit her more—" he blurted out, as flat and cold as I had ever heard him speak to anyone.

"I was going to go. I had plans to go." Her name was right there, I told him, boxed off in my *New Yorker* desk calendar—Saturday morning, 10 a.m.: CLETA!

"You should have gone *regularly,* Kelly. She was your grandmother." I started to cry, first from shame, then from a kind of secondary shame that I was crying from shame rather than grief.

"When are you coming down?" I asked.

"Later today. We'll call you back." As he hung up, busy and mad, I threw out a weak "I'm sorry" but he didn't hear me and it wasn't the time for that, anyway. He had a eulogy to write, a Buick to fill with gasoline, a dozen phone calls to make.

I slipped away from my desk to the only single bathroom in the office. I locked the door, lowered the toilet lid, and sat down to bawl. I had let Greenie down. I had been immature and self-centered and he had noticed and there was no making up for it. I vowed to be a model child from now on—anticipating needs, asking for assignments, showing up early and properly dressed.

By the time my parents arrived that evening, Baltimore had called home all its Corrigans. We were now fifty-six by birth and twenty-odd more by marriage. We met at Ocean Pride on York Road. The menu was dominated by what Maryland considers to be the pride of the ocean: crabs. Crab fluff, soft-shell crabs, crab cakes, crab nachos, crab pretzels/soup/balls: you get the idea. In the back room, we sat at long tables picking hard crabs rolled in Old Bay seasoning and downing cold light beer from scuffed plastic pitchers. Riffs of "Super Freak" wafted in from the bar.

Eventually, the toasts began. Aunt Mary talked about "Mother's" gift for gab, her cooking, and her faith. Uncle Jimmy talked about her iron will and the wrangling it took to get that many kids through school. Greenie stood next. Cleta was tough as nails: "When she had to, she could give a helluva spanking." She was resourceful and creative, persevering and loyal. She was "family first." I bowed my head. *Family first.* Had I learned nothing?

I went to sleep that night thinking about how funny and approachable "St. Cleta" sounded and how easy it would have been to pop in for five-minute fly-bys on my way to Fells Point for Jägermeister Thursdays.

At her wake, held at an Irish funeral home, we spent several hours at the viewing. Eventually, after an hour with the casket in my peripheral vision, I walked over and looked in. There she was, dressed in a blue wool A-line dress and thick hose, her purple-y hairdo swept up—as ever—off her forehead, her veiny hands that had done so much cooking and sewing and bottom-smacking now crossed gently over her Mrs. Claus chest. I was taken with the papery quality of her skin. I wanted to touch it but didn't dare; the fine cracks in its surface made her seem delicate, countering her legendary toughness. I wondered if that had happened since she died or in her final year.

Her funeral was held the next morning at the Cathedral of Mary Our Queen on Charles Street, a structure so vast Johnny Unitas himself couldn't have thrown a football from one end to the other. The first four pews were crammed with her children, her grandchildren, and a few dozen great-grandchildren, hair combed or curled. Perfume and hairspray mingled with the incense and must of the cathedral. I wore a rayon ensemble from The Limited, a massive khaki skirt and matching jacket with sharp, dramatic shoulders, a trend set in motion by people like Iman and David Byrne. Behind us sat several hundred of Baltimore's Catholic mafia. Everyone cried for Cleta, and maybe for other things too. It was not lost on me that for the first time, my father and his siblings were now in the pew closest to the altar.

On the steps of the church, family and friends stood tall in wool suits and dark dresses. Cigarettes were lit. Women pulled on black leather gloves. There was hugging and laughing and remembrances, faces that hadn't been seen in decades. My cousins had so many Cleta stories— driving her to church, bringing their friends to see her, the time she drank a little too much scotch. I was outside the circle in a way I hated. I wove in and out, looking for Greenie, tracking him. We weren't right yet, but he wasn't thinking about me. His mother had died.

Cars eventually streamed from the parking lot to the "back-after" where I killed a sixer of Bud Light and smoked at least half a pack of my cousin Trey's Merits. We sang our family song, my brothers flanking my dad. *C-O-double-R-I-G-A-N spells Corrigan, proud of all the Irish blood that's in me, never a man to say a word ag'in' me . . .* We ate ham and a Campbell's soup casserole with cornflakes on top and sang "God Bless America."

The day after the funeral, the Originals returned to the cathedral for 9:30 mass without their spouses, who were packing hard plastic suitcases in bedrooms all over Baltimore and feeding their kids, who had more than met their weekly quota for worship. I tagged along with Greenie, still wanting to find a way back in. We sat in Cleta's pew. He didn't even know I was there.

My need for relief did not trump Greenie's need to grieve. If the stirring lasted for days, well, I would have to sit in my regret like cold bathwater until he could turn his attention to secondary concerns. There is an intrinsic order to everything and that order will be honored. First you fill the car with gas then you check traffic on the radio then you slide up and down the dials until you find the Orioles game. First you visit your grandmother then you hit the weekly diet confab then you race down Pratt Street to catch the gang at Half Price Wings Night.

When mass ended, the seven of us took two cars back to my other grandmother's house on Tunbridge Road. Libby greeted everyone tenderly. She was fond of Cleta. My mother came downstairs to greet the crowd assembled around the glossy walnut dining table. She looked pretty and sure, like she knew what to do. I mirrored her posture. She filled coffees and told me to pass the hot cross buns and make sure everyone got a napkin.

After some gushing over the pastries, Uncle Dickie got to telling an old story about some pet chickens they had when they were kids and lived, for a while when finances were particularly thin, in the country. It took four of them to remember the chickens' names: Barney and Jerry. I said I couldn't imagine a world where barnyard fowl could double as pets, which made it clear I was the only one in the room who didn't know the story (even Libby had heard it), so I became the audience.

"Kel, there was a dog next door," Dickie said. "What was his name?"

"The ugliest mutt you ever saw," Greenie jumped in, looking right at me, which felt glorious. "Pepper!"

"Yes! Pepper! Good God, I hated that dog."

They were indistinguishable, the six of them, each tossing in little chips of the story, making a big pile in the middle.

"Pepper got in our yard and went after the chickens, chasing them around the yard, until—"

"Oh my God, Dickie ran out there, tears streaming down his cheeks. He was distraught! He said—" My dad struggled to speak through his hysterics. "He said we should put them back together and bury them!"

"But, leave it to Cleta"—Gene looked at me—"to gather up the mess and make chicken cacciatore."

The Originals exploded with laughter.

"Cleta would have no sooner buried good food, Lovey—" Greenie put his hand on top of my arm. Our separation was over. "And oh my God, Dickie *wailed,* straight through dinner."

The remembering left them winded, like kids

playing tag. After another round of sighs, a period of recovery and eye-blotting, Gene said, "By God, she could cook. Cleta Corrigan could *cook*."

A weekend of memorializing Cleta was wrapping up. My parents would be heading back to Philly in a few minutes. It was time.

I found Greenie out by the car, situating luggage in the trunk.

"Well," he started.

"I feel terrible, Dad." He turned to face me. "I should have gone to see Cleta more. I was wrong, I was selfish."

"It's important. When people get old, it's hard. It's an important thing to get right, Kelly." I nodded. "Now you know."

"Now I know," I said, tears rising.

"And she was such a great lady."

I nodded again.

"Okay, Lovey, hand me that cooler."

Maybe being wrong is not the same as being bad, I thought, not a sign that your insides were rotten. Maybe you can still be a decent-ish person, a person with a personal mission statement, a person who aspires to be someone habitually good and highly effective, and fuck up.

What took me much longer to understand is that to love someone is to love the people they love, or at least, *try*. It's so obvious to me now: my father wasn't asking me to keep a regular visitation schedule with Cleta as if she were my dentist. He was asking me to know her, to enjoy her, not to let her go to waste. That was my mistake. *I'm sorry I missed her, Greenie. I was wrong not to know her.*

I kissed my parents goodbye and drove home to my apartment, wondering about my future, the kids I would someday have and the awkward or easy ways they might relate to Greenie and my mom. Would they visit my parents? Would they want to? Would it matter to them that it mattered to me? And would I forgive their predictable indifference?

I would, of course, because the being-wrong business never ends. I would forgive my someday-children nearly as often as I would need forgiveness from them. Together, we would practice a circular, ongoing amnesty. It would be required.

Good Enough

Many of the smart-sounding things I say are lifted from conversations with my friend Ariel. Every Tuesday morning, we drop our kids off at school and walk a one-hour loop around Piedmont. She likes to take the hills, during which she can talk without ever sounding breathless. (She is much younger than I am.) I like her because she asks smart questions, remembers everything you tell her, and emerged whole from a childhood that would make you blanch. Also, she knows and can explain tons of stuff about people and the way they work, not only because she is naturally observant and has Dalai Lama–level emotional IQ but also because Ariel is also Dr. Trost, psychotherapist. She listens, professionally, thirty hours a week in an office over a bookstore on College Avenue.

She'd wanted to be a therapist since her first psych class in high school. A few weeks in, she found herself doing extra homework, which led to an interest in trauma, which led her to conduct an astonishing independent study: interviewing women who'd been through sexual assault. "From that moment on, I never considered any other career," she said.

She did her undergrad at UC Berkeley, and two

years later started in the Ph.D. program at UT Austin. After one year of classwork and study, something called practicum begins, during which students accumulate the three thousand hours of patient interaction required for licensing. In other words, upon completing nine classes, students advance from interviewing people to treating them. Ariel couldn't yet imagine herself in the role. "I was terrified. I would have studied for five more years before I'd have felt ready."

Practicum was set to begin on the campus of a small progressive Catholic university near UT known as St. Ed's that offered special programs to African refugees. Ariel told her instructor she couldn't do it. Her mentor in the program, a fortyish mother of two named Laura, asked Ariel to describe her concerns. "Being a charlatan," Ariel said. Laura—who had both professional credentials and, because of a violent attack that left her partially disfigured, tremendous personal credibility—assured Ariel repeatedly that she was sufficiently prepared.

Ariel looked down at her diamond engagement ring. "Should I take this off? I mean, really, how dare I have this?"

"For all you know," Laura said, "that ring suggests you have a lot of education, that you are an established person who has the personal support that makes you able to support others."

Ariel was unconvinced. "What does twenty-four-year-old, well-educated, well-fed, well-loved me have to draw on? Books? Class exercises? Why should these people trust me with their stories, their suffering?"

"Because you're trustworthy, and being trustworthy is enough."

Ariel was paired with a woman from Sierra Leone who called herself Jean.

"Jean was small and in her twenties," Ariel said, "but she was a grown-ass woman." Their conversations began with a series of basic assessments: Are you experiencing anxiety? Has your appetite changed? How much alcohol do you consume per week? In session, Jean was quiet and deferential. She was the mother of a three-year-old. She worked nights on an assembly line for a computer manufacturing company. It took time for Ariel to learn that Jean's boss was nasty, a screamer. During the day, Jean was redoing years of coursework she had completed in her native country so that she might someday regain her professional status; in Sierra Leone, Jean had been an engineer.

Between sessions with Jean, Ariel met with Laura, who continued to assure her that she was up to the work. "Laura was the first person to say, 'You don't need to be something you aren't. You're good enough.'"

Slowly, over the course of a year, Jean told Ariel that her entire family had been killed in the genocide. And she had been raped. Jean and her son, a child of that assault, were alone in Texas. Jean talked about raising a child in a foreign country, about the unrelenting stress of living in survival mode, about what it feels like to be at the mercy of an angry man.

Over dozens of sessions, Ariel rose into the job, becoming the very thing Laura assured her she was, which was both less and more than Ariel expected. "I think I was the first person ever to listen to her," Ariel said, "to hear the whole story, to take it in. I think that was enough."

Recently, Ariel's daughter, Ruby, was bat mitzvahed.

The stuff Jewish people expect a brand-new teenager to pull off during a bat or bar mitzvah is—well, let's just say, I started taking a second language around the same age and wasn't expected to speak or sing, forward or backward, from memory or page, alone or in front of a crowd for a good six years. And French has *vowels*.

The preparation, as you might know, involves several years of weekly Hebrew school and tutorials in addition to one-on-one meetings with a rabbi—in Ruby's case, a tiny, bright-voiced woman named Noa. Ruby was also required to complete a mitzvah—a major community service project. Horse-obsessed, Ruby created a scholarship program called Take the Reins for underprivileged kids to take lessons at the barn where she rides. "Caring for animals is proven to make people more empathetic," I heard her explain to Claire.

The day arrived. We squeezed in a pew and watched, for ninety minutes, as Ruby sang in Hebrew and told stories from the Old Testament. Ruby was beyond composed; she was commanding. Noa stood behind her, delighted but not surprised. Toward the end of the service, Ruby delivered a *drash,* a sermon to the congregation, something not even nuns—grown women who study the word of God every day—are allowed to do in the religion of my childhood. My daughters—more familiar with JoJo and Jordan from *The Bachelorette* than with Jacob and Joseph from the Bible—were flabbergasted.

It was clear to me that day in San Francisco that a bat mitzvah is really one mighty chorus of *You are good enough.* That's what Ruby was being told—by her parents when they said that they looked forward to watching "the continued unfolding of her beautiful life," by her grandparents, by Rabbi Noa, who represented Ruby's entire faith, and by us, her incredulous friends. *You are good enough,* we said in unison, meaning: good enough to take on nothing less than the rest of your life.

After the ceremony, I ended up in conversation

with Rabbi Noa's husband, Rabbi Michael, who guides about fifty thirteen-year-olds through their bat and bar mitzvahs every year. We talked for an hour. He has a hundred stories he loves telling and it was immediately clear that he had found his vocation; his faith flooded the conversation.

I started by asking why the event is tagged to turning thirteen. "Thirteen is a pivotal moment, and not just because of mustaches and curves. It's a time of explosive intellectual and emotional growth. But it's also when life tends to get treacherous. They are going into the eye of the hurricane. We want our faith, our community, to help them find and feel their own power." What he meant by *power* was specifically the power to participate meaningfully in the world, not as a needy child but as a force for good.

I asked Rabbi Michael if there were ever kids he worried over, kids who weren't up to the demands of the ceremony and all it implied. "The hit rate, so far as I've seen, is a hundred percent," he said. "By which I mean there is always growth, there is always a rise." He said one of his favorite bat mitzvah moments was when a mother was holding the microphone to her daughter's lips and the daughter took the mike and said, *"Mom, I got it."*

"I love to see a kid feel the weight of the moment, to see them understand that they have something to say, that their voice deserves to be amplified. Grabbing the mike? That was too perfect."

One of the "white-hot holiest days" of his life was the bat mitzvah of Gabriela, a fifteen-year-old girl in a wheelchair who loved Green Day, horses, and Tolkien. Gabriela had Rett syndrome, a genetic neurological disorder that involves seizures, GI problems, and often an inability to speak, as was the case with Gabriela. Nonetheless, working with her indomitable mother, Harriet, and a device that Gabriela could control with her chin to enable herself to type, she completed the same course of preparation that Ruby did.

On the day of Gabriela's bat mitzvah, she weighed thirty-eight pounds. "She was bubbling with holiness," Michael remembered. " 'God is everywhere in everyone,' her machine-voice said." He took a deep breath. "I can close my eyes and be back in that morning, in that moment. There's no greater gift than to help a child see their enoughness, their might."

At thirteen, I was into Carly Simon, *Charlie's Angels,* and Minute Rice with butter and salt. I didn't have a worldview or my own nonprofit, but my teachers liked me and I didn't lie that much to my parents. By fifteen, I had fallen into a groove—and not a good one.

Sophomore year started okay. I had landed a

four-dollar-an-hour gig at Villanova Pizza, giving me access to free calzones and a college freshman named Matt who was deadly cute but very short, a weakness I thought gave me, and my brand-new boobs that I caught him looking at more than once, a shot. I went to work in painstakingly chosen outfits—stonewashed single-pleat jeans, an alligator shirt, my transparent Swatch, and Tretorns. I talked about anything I could think of that would make me seem older: concerts I was planning to see, hanging out with my brother at Washington and Lee. Before I could close the deal, Stubby, the manager, called me into the crummy back office. After observing me for five shifts, he said, he had no choice but to fire me. Apparently, I didn't take my work seriously, as I had proved by showing up late, taking excessive smoke breaks, and asking phone-ins to wait while I finished another jokey exchange with Matt. *Oh my God, I'm a loser,* I thought, an estimation that I suspect was shared by my brothers, neither of whom had ever been fired, and my mother, though she wouldn't have phrased it in those terms.

But then there was Greenie—who laughed.

"It's not funny, I'm a loser."

"No, you're not. You'll figure it out. You've got what it takes, kid." What could he possibly be seeing in me?

Not one month later, after I'd been cut from the

field hockey team and mounted a failed campaign for student government, I went shoplifting at Sears, wandering from department to department, snatching goodies, until an undercover security guy grabbed my elbow. Back in the office, the officer unpacked eighteen items totaling $56 from my backpack: candy, fake jewelry, control-top pantyhose for my mother's upcoming birthday. Later that spring, I found myself in a weeklong in-school suspension for being spaghetti-leg drunk at the sophomore semi-formal. I did my time next to kids who had vandalized lockers and given teachers the finger *to their faces*. I was one of them now, Winona Ryder crossed with Lindsay Lohan. I wanted to be someone better—class secretary and captain of the lacrosse team—not Rejected Candidate, Failed Athlete, Unemployed Pizza Girl, Petty Thief.

During this bang-up year, my mother aged a decade while Greenie, ever faithful, just kept shrugging. He'd come up to my room after work, his tie loose around his neck, a can of Miller Lite in his hand. Sitting on my canopy bed, surrounded by pink-and-white gingham wallpaper laughably incongruous with the derelict who lived there, he'd ask about my latest transgression. I'd blather about my failures, my regrets, my sinking fortunes.

"This is all part of growing up. You're all right, Lovey."

"No, I'm not."

"You're good enough," he'd say, patting my knee. "Trust me."

Back at school, passing student government meetings and listening to announcements about upcoming field hockey games, *You're good enough* were the only words I had to combat my deep intuition, to say nothing of the mounting evidence, that I was defective.

In college, shortly after I was called in front of the Panhellenic Council for throwing a sorority happy hour that involved shots for all, even for the official who'd been sent by National to monitor our fledgling chapter, I was fired again, this time from my job as a cashier in the dining hall. A nice man who had worked on campus for years said I was his first-ever "termination," but what choice did he have after learning that I was giving away Snickers bars to fraternity presidents, soccer players, and our school's most celebrated exchange student, a lanky, doe-eyed Italian named Matteo who was so *mozzafiato* I was tempted to throw my undies in there too. In the fall of senior year, I topped off my college career with a DUI that required I spend the night in jail with a hooker named Oz and, in the morning, hand over my driver's license for six months.

After college, I missed more milestones and made new messes. Twenty-seven pounds overweight, I drank coffee all day and smoked half a pack of cigarettes every night. By thirty, when most of my friends had celebrated their first anniversary and several had become homeowners, I was single and $6,000 in debt. I had yet to take self-care seriously. A mole I ignored turned into an invasive melanoma. But Greenie, blind to the flaws of his beloveds and, I learned, a bit of a late bloomer himself, dismissed my plunging trend line. "I'm telling you, Lovey, you're gonna get there." *Where? When?* I wondered.

Finally, ten years later, after I'd set up a decent life as a functional forty-year-old, after I had become something closer to the person he always thought I would be, I asked Greenie why he had been so sure I'd sort it out. "You know, Lovey, you were never down for long. You'd get cut from field hockey and try out for cheerleading. And then that didn't work and you did chorus or the diving team. You don't need to get it right every time, you know what I mean? A couple wins here and there is plenty."

That's how it works: someone important believes in us, loudly and with conviction and against all substantiation, and over time, we begin to believe, too—not in our shot at perfection, mind you, but in the *good enough* version of us that they have reflected. The mentors and rabbis, the grannies on the bema, are certain about things we can't yet believe: that listening is huge, that there's might in the act of committing yourself to a cause, that trying again is both all we can do and our great enabling power. They see clearly that *we* weren't wrong; our aim was. They know that we are good enough, as we are, with not much more than our hopeful, honorable intent to keep at it. They tell us, over and over, until we can hear it.

My mother had been out to California to visit us in our new home, which I had creatively appointed with DIY "furniture" that only later became embarrassing. She stayed for four days. The first night, I took her to an Italian place in North Beach. She was impressed both with the food and the prices, and wowed by my parallel parking. The next night we had friends over. She liked the snack plate I put out, and thought I was smart to give the girls little bowls of cut bell peppers and cherry tomatoes before I handed over the macaroni and cheese. Over coffee the next day, I made a store list, sorted the recycling, took a call about the school fundraiser, made a doctor's appointment, filled sippy cups with orange juice cut with water, found a shoe. I did my life and she watched.

On the car ride to the airport she sighed and said, "Well, Kelly, I'll tell you this: you're nothing if not competent." I nearly cried. Sure, Greenie had effused about my potential a hundred times before, but my mother's appraisal was based on verifiable observation. It was a declaration of what she considered a fact.

If you want to know the truth, I've never thought of myself quite the same since. Me: *nothing if not competent.* Me and my little life: *good enough.*

I Love You

I remember kind of swooning when I learned how the French say it: *Je t'adore*. I was in high school and the phrase brought to mind kitten heels, martinis, and open-mouth kissing. But really, when you're a grown-up, *I love you* is more romantic than the perfumy *Je t'adore*. Informed love, love that has cut across time and thwarted its pressures, is a two-ton emotion, and the plain, full statement of it often makes my throat clog with feeling.

I love you is not *I love your giggle and mysterious expressions* or *I love the way your bra matches your panties*. It's *Even though your neck dropped into a wattle last year and you burp a lot after you eat Thai food and have not conquered your social insecurities and I heard you yell sharply at our kids* again *and you still can't seem to bring yourself to be nicer to my mom or ask for that raise, I love you.*

As for the rest of our permanent relationships, where people know each other too well, I find it nearly incomprehensible that, in spite of every offense and oversight, we can still say *I love you* and mean it. I believe this emotional largesse is sometimes called forgiveness. Immediate, often unsolicited, sometimes undeserved forgiveness—

that is what turns the wheel of family life.

We forgive: Our parents, for being wrong about us in so many ways, for seeing some things and not others, for missing the point. Our siblings, for being smarter or more athletic or happier than we are. Our children, for diverging from our expectations, for scaring us with their developmentally appropriate but still dreadful risk taking, for growing up and leaving and forgetting to call. Ourselves, for being less than we planned when we were young and dreamed of outer space and Olympic medals. Such sprawling deficiency—ours, theirs, ever more varieties and degrees as each new day passes—to be acknowledged, to be pardoned. And yet, we do. We love and are loved anyway. Differently, though, than we might have thought.

From parent to teenager, *I love you* is not *I love the way our interactions leave me feeling useful and appreciated and like I am definitely in the top percentile of parents working today.* It's *Even though I delivered you at permanent expense to my genitals and you rolled your eyes at me when I tried to hit the dab, and you trapped me in that modern-day torture chamber of club music and olfactory assault, Abercrankie and Filth, then later that day, impatient to be taken to Bridget's house, you beeped at me from the passenger seat in the driveway, like maybe I worked for you, I love you.*

Or from one sibling to another, *I love you* is not *I love the way we instantly make sense to each other and fall into plans effortlessly and always remember each other's birthdays.* It's *Even though we hardly agree about a thing, including who should be president, how often we should call each other, or even where to get hoagies, I love you.*

Or from a middle-aged woman to her mother, *I love you* is not *I love how we share clothes and taste in movies and concur on all aspects of raising a girl circa 2017.* It's *Even though every time we talk, you tell me Joan Jennings's hearing is shot and ask me if I saw what Mark Cuban said on* Shark Tank *or if you should get a Roku or why your avatar in Netflix is a purple raccoon and then we pretend you might one day come out to California again even though it's been five years and we both know you're never getting on a plane again, I love you.*

Or to a dying parent—in this case, a father—*I love you* is not *I love your spot-on career advice or how you always give it to me straight.* It's *Even though you said you were feeling better after I smoothed your cornsilk hair and put a pill way back on your tongue and cleaned your dentures under the running water and changed your diaper, even though I begged you not to leave—or if you had to leave, to just open your eyes one more time—and you left anyway, and I*

can't find you anywhere except on my answering
machine where your boyish voice is asking me if
we caught the last play of the Notre Dame game,
I love you.

The first time the words pass between two people: electrifying.

Ten thousand times later: cause for marvel.

The last time: the dream you revisit over and over and over again.

No Words at All

When witnessing virtuosity—a Steph Curry finger roll in traffic, or my friend Cava directing the Oakland School for the Arts choir with her eyes closed—what good are clunky words? That's why facial expressions were invented. And cheers, dance moves, high fives, embraces, and emojis.

The other problem with language is that arranging words into sentences requires we flip on our thinking machine, which necessarily claims some of our focus, so that as soon as we start deciding how to explain a feeling, we're not entirely feeling the feeling anymore, and some feelings want to be felt at full capacity.

That's why, after Liz died, I didn't want to talk to anyone. I just wanted to sit and feel, often with my hand over my mouth, often closing my eyes and shaking my head for no one. She had limped through the last month of her life on Percocet and fentanyl, trying to hold on until Christmas, which she had planned to manage as she always had: by prioritizing gratitude and togetherness over list-making and consumption. Then she was gone and the phone starting ringing. A week later, I owed a dozen people phone calls, friends who had heard the awful news and wanted to connect.

I ached for some of them—losing a friend makes the others more dear—but I couldn't call them back. I tried with my friend Julie, but there was this thing that happened, a nutshelling, that made me feel cheap and phony. She said *She fought hard.* I said *At least she has no more pain.* Julie said I had been *a great comfort* to Liz. The conversation was loving, and banal, and pitiful. We tidied what should not be tidied, because who can sit with all that awfulness unspooled around them? And anyway, it was *a phone call.* One person says something and the other person says something else. You don't just breathe into your receivers at each other.

There was another risk, that I'd call someone back and we wouldn't talk about Liz *enough.* I'd find myself taking an interest in something other than her, like a son's basketball injury or a disturbing spate of sexting between teenagers. What if I lost track of her for a second? What if I accidentally cared about someone's kitchen remodel or which iPhone to get? Then I was just like everyone else on the bus, thinking my me thoughts, too feeble to hold the grief pose for even a couple of weeks.

There was a third problem. Liz had been sick off and on since 2009; people had been getting ready. Those people, post-emotion, would punctuate the conversation with move-along words like *well.* I hated *well,* the way it lured the word *anyway* to the lips. *Those poor kids* made my skin crawl, the way *those* put the *poor kids* at a distance. And fuck *Fuck cancer* and its false gutsiness, the way it'd been graphically designed into a perfect square, for easy Instagramming. Nobody who has cancer says *Fuck cancer,* unless they're playing Spunky Patient for someone who hasn't had cancer.

Surely, my friend, my lost and lovely friend, called for new words. For a while I'd say she'd been *robbed* or *ripped off.* After the potency of the crime metaphor wore off, I turned to the vocabulary of religion. *It's a sin. It's hell.* Then the ocean with its *waves,* so *vast,* impossible to touch bottom. Then a maze, then a mountain, then seasons, a natural disaster. I never came up with any combination that came close to the feeling. Despair defies description. Ask the dancers and the athletes, the painters and musicians, ask anyone who has participated in a moment of silence: the reach of language can be laughable.

The summer before Liz died, our families met in Big Sky, Montana, for a week of hikes, whitewater rafting, and dinners at a long table. As usual, she was focused on her kids, tracking their moods, scanning for hazards, catching them before they fell into a fit. She was the world's expert on these three people; she could read their body language like a radar weather map.

Before dinner on the last night, while the guys were on the deck drinking whiskey and talking about Elon Musk, Liz and I went on a walk and she told me about a dream she'd been fixating on, a dream about what happens after mothers die.

"We are all in this place. All the mothers who had to leave early." (I would repeat her unforgettable phrasing—*had to leave early*—to Edward as we went to sleep that night.) "It's huge, big as an airplane hangar, and there are all these seats, rows and rows, set up on a glass floor, so all the moms can look down and watch their kids live out their futures." How dominant the ache to know what becomes of our children. "There's one rule: you can watch as much and as long as you want, but you can only intervene once."

I nodded, tears forming.

"So I sat down. And I watched. I watched them out back by the pool, swimming with Andy, napping on a towel. I watched them on the jungle gym, walking Lambchop, reading their Lemony Snicket books. I watched Margo taking a wrong turn or forgetting her homework. I watched Dru ignoring his coach. I watched Gwennie logging her feelings in a journal. And every time I went to intervene, to warn one of the kids about something or just pick them up to hold them, a more experienced mother leaned across and stopped me. *Not now. He'll figure it out. She'll come around.* And it went on and on like that and in the end," she said, smiling with wet eyes, "I never needed to use my interventions."

Her dream was that she had, in her too-short lifetime, endowed her children with everything they'd require to negotiate the successive obstacle courses of adolescence, young adulthood, and grown-up life.

"I mean, they had heartaches and regret and fights and broken bones," she said, stopping to rest. "They made tons of mistakes, but they didn't need *me*. I never had to say anything or stop anything. I never said one word." She put her arm through mine and we started moving again, back toward the house, touching from our shoulders to our elbows, crunching the gravel with our steps, the mingled voices of our children coming from the door we left open.

Once a week I take off all my jewelry, slip into a shapeless blue polyester volunteer coat, clip ID tags to my lapel, and drive 5.3 miles through Piedmont and down 52nd Street to our local children's hospital. I park, take the elevator to the third floor, and buzz myself into the NICU. Standing at a wall of metal sinks, I scrub up to my elbows for a full minute, enjoying the smell of the soap and the sound the brush makes against my fingernails. I dry off, gown up, and walk the nurseries, listening for babies in distress.

Sometimes all three rooms are calm. Forty-some infants sleeping off heart surgery or recovering from traumatic births or growing their lungs. Some of the preemies, smaller than the bag of medicine being dripped into them, are in clear plastic isolation units. Some babies have been there for months.

In the year or so since I started volunteering, it's never taken more than a few minutes for a nurse to wave me over and pair me with a baby.

In the beginning, I worried about offending the mothers. Surely, they would not want an anonymous woman holding their fragile angels? But they do. They all do. Few can afford— financially, logistically, or emotionally—to be at the hospital day after day when a baby needs to stay in the NICU for weeks or months. Most have jobs they have to go back to, both for the paycheck and for the health insurance. Many have older children who need meals and rides and attention. Other families live so far away they can only come every other day. Some moms are teenagers who go to high school or community college. And a handful of moms are drug addicts who will never come back to collect their babies. Even those, maybe especially those, want their babies to be held.

Though I'm always curious to know the details of their traumas and conditions, privacy laws forbid all reference to personal or medical information with volunteers. It wouldn't be useful anyway, not to the babies, who I am there to serve. As in most situations, it's not important why someone hurts, only that they do.

A longtime staffer named Bette trained me over several weeks.

Bette is a small woman with curly gray hair and blue eyes. For thirty-five years, she's been teaching new parents how to hold their baby, how to massage, swaddle, nurse, and bathe. She has a refined eye for body language and knows things about silence and its special comforts. She doesn't look at every day like a project; she doesn't need progress to report. She is there to settle. To soothe. Achievements in the NICU are of the most subtle sort.

I hold the babies like Bette taught me to, attentive to their micro movements—tension in the forehead, a swatting motion, rooting into my chest (as if there might be one more silky ounce left). I pore over swirls of hair, on their heads and cheeks and arms, little *Starry Night*s of the finest silk. I ponder fingers and knuckles and nails. I study hairlines—peninsulas, cowlicks, low on the forehead or squared off as if by a ruler. I wonder if their lips, so thin now, will unfurl as Claire's did, or if their hair, so dark, will turn gold later, surprising everyone. When I am sure it won't disturb them, I remove tiny flakes of dried skin from their ears.

The lights are dim. The nurses whisper.

The monitors chirp and ping. The babies rest. My long big-lung breaths stretch underneath three of theirs.

If they're awake, the babies don't always look at me. They fixate on a light or a spot in the distance or a nearby mobile. But last week a baby boy with a swollen head and a shunt near his temple found my eyes and locked in. We stared at each other, blinking back and forth, each blink longer than the last, until he could hold his lids open no longer and the rows of his dark glossy eyelashes came together like a Venus flytrap. Bette, who had been watching from across the room, nodded at me and winked. He'd rest on my chest for the next hour, my heartbeat, my warmth and humanity an incalculable improvement on his indifferent crib. The skin hungers for touch, from cradle to grave.

"Close silence—that's all they need," she whispered to me.

Georgia once asked me if we really needed to talk so much on the ride home from school. She was happy to see me but wondered if she could be excused from showing it. She had talked all day, answered every adult's every question and found a clever response to every dumb boy's taunt and quip. By 3:45, she was ready to stare out the window and say nothing.

On the days I sit with the babies, I'm better

at the close silence parenting often requires. My needs diminish. I am less outside my life, critiquing it, and more *in* it, moving quietly, even reverently, through its spaces, awed by the way two people—even a gung-ho mother and her tapped-out teenager—can hold each other without touching and cheer each other without saying a word.

Onward

Dear Liz,

I'm writing from my chair in the nook off the kitchen where I always sat when we were on the phone. It's been a year and a half since you were alive.

We're just back from being with Andy and the kids. We've seen them a lot. I think five times in the last year. Edward flew down a couple of days after you died. He took a cab to your house and when he came through the laundry room door, Andy and the kids were in the kitchen, at the table, stamping and addressing holiday cards. They sent out two hundred and twenty-five. The card said, "Counting Blessings." Lambchop got a cameo on the back. When Edward got home he said to me, "Are we sure we 'don't have the energy' to send cards this year?"

When your birthday came around in June, we went down to your house for a long weekend. The Lowes came too. We had kringle in the morning and spaghetti with your sauce that night. No one lifted a fork until the last person was at the table. They held hands and paused before they dug in. They said, *Thank you for the food before us, the people around us, and the love between us.* They said it fast like it meant nothing but it's your line and they knew it and they felt it and so did we. We listened to a playlist from your phone (which Andy has in his pocket all the time). The Alabama Shakes, that "Cotton Eyed Joe" song, Billie Holiday. We told stories, like the one Dru likes about the time you killed a spider in the bathroom without blinking and the day you found a snake in the canoe. We sat outside at a long table and gave each other small presents you would have liked. Funny socks, a shiny plastic wallet, a journal. We took our time. Each gift was passed around. We let ourselves feel our connections, our gratitude, you. We decided to make it an annual tradition.

The next day, I caught Andy in the kitchen making beet juice with the kids. He took out your giant metal juicing machine, the one that irked him so. The girls fed purple beets and ginger root and cucumber through the grinder. Dru dumped out the pulp. They clinked their little glasses, the ones with colored bicycles you kept on the low shelf by the sink. Andy saw me across the kitchen simpering and said, "Yeah, yeah, I know." They drank it all, Liz. They had beet-juice mustaches.

That afternoon, we all went to watch Gwen play baseball. When she took off her batting helmet and that white hair fell out, she was so you I shivered. She and Margo still move in tandem. They read all the same books and sleep next to each other at night.

A month later, the kids went to Camp Kesem in San Diego. They loved it. Their camp names were M&M, Kit Kat, and Tic Tac. They're signed up already for this summer. They'll do it every year, I bet, and when they get to college, they'll become counselors—the most compassionate counselors.

Our Thanksgiving tradition continues. Your gang came to us this time. Andy brought the string of gratitude flags we made with you the year before. He had kept it in a cardboard envelope so it wouldn't get bent. I helped him hang it up in the dining room. The kids loved seeing it again; they laughed at sloppy penmanship and at how one of the kids misspelled *thanful* but not *scientists fighting cancer*. I gasped when I saw your handwriting. It felt like you must be close by. We said a long grace. We toasted the great people we'd met since the year before.

After dinner, Gwennie had a tummyache. I took her up to my room and we squeezed into a chair together. We'd spent the day with a big group and I asked her if it was hard to hear all the other kids saying *My mom says we can get double dessert . . . . I better ask my mom. . . . Mom, can we watch Nemo after dinner?* Gwen nodded and we cried together, and then half an hour later she threw up and I wondered if I had misread the situation and compounded a physical problem with emotions. I'm so sorry if I did.

In the morning while we were eating breakfast, Edward gave a speech to the kids about how you should only ever fry bacon in a cast-iron pan and I rolled my eyes and Andy joked, "Embrace the idiosyncrasies." Edward snapped at me later that day for changing the afternoon plan too many times and Andy put his hands on the kitchen counter to calm himself and said, "Seriously, guys, embrace the idiosyncrasies." He hasn't whitewashed your marriage; he remembers the conflict, the push-pull. He says the struggle is what made your marriage *your* marriage. He can have his way on everything now but about half the time, he does it your way anyway.

We were all together recently at your place in Montana. Edward and I took the master, Andy made us. He slept with Dru on that big mattress in the nook. The girls had the bunk room downstairs. So many things went right.

Dru, a big ten-year-old, is impossibly lean and muscular and gorgeous. Maybe he's just growing up or maybe it's to do with you but we played Yahtzee and he lost and it was no problem. He's still a madman on the slopes, always first to the bottom, but he makes turns and seems more controlled in every way. When I look at him, Liz, you are right there and I swear to God he knows it. He knows I'm looking at you and he loves it. He holds my gaze, he lets me fall in. There's something about his skin, his eyes; he's lit from within.

Margo is settled in her new school. Ninth grade next year. She's getting busier. Volleyball, parties, days at the beach. She started lacrosse this year. We sent her some mesh pinnies. Her mind still wanders. She gets that dreamy look, and I laugh, thinking about how happy it would make you that she hasn't changed, that loss didn't snap her out of herself.

Gwennie is ready to finish sixth grade and be at Pacific Ridge with Margo next year. She is planning her twelfth birthday; she wants to go to a library. I know, so perfect. The three of us talked on the ski lift together this winter. Smart girls. Deep. Gwen was wearing your purple helmet. It felt okay to say that they would look so good in your clothes. They smiled. I said, "You're lucky your mom had such great style; my kids wouldn't touch my stretch khakis." They laughed. I regretted saying "You're lucky."

That afternoon, when we came in from snowboarding, Gwen let me hold her for a long time. I was lying on your couch in long johns in front of a fire Edward made and Andy fixed. I reached out my arms and she came over and got on top of me and I held her for you, for as long as she would let me. Two songs at least. Then Margo announced it was time to make brownies and she was gone. It was sublime.

On the morning we left, I French-braided Margo's hair while Andy watched. He said he had tried to learn but the girls could do it better by themselves. Dru said we forgot to play our Happy Family game and we said next time. We hugged and everyone said, "I love you," which we always do now.

Andy spent a lot of time thinking about how to handle December 12, the first-year anniversary. He decided to start what will be an annual tradition involving stories and photos. He asked five of us—your sister, your parents, me, Jessica, and Jen—to find a picture of you and write a couple paragraphs about it. He coached us to be specific. He found durable screw-post binders and bought four, so that he and each of the kids could have their own, wherever they go, forever. I talked about your easy athleticism because I remember you saying how much you hated that your kids might only think of you as the feeble woman wrapped in blankets on the couch. I told them you were the best athlete I ever knew.

The albums will grow each year. The five of us will keep sharing one photo and one small story and that's how your family will spend the day you died, because Andy wants to remind them of things they might have forgotten or been too young and distracted to notice, and as they get older and can understand the more complex adult parts of you, he wants them to keep getting to know you. I was there a month later for a quick one-night visit and he had the binders sitting out on the counter. He handed me one and we went through each page. "It really went great," he said. "We were—*happy*." And they were, that day and many other days.

I know it doesn't end, being motherless. I know you will never stop *not being there*. But your kids are connected and Andy keeps space for them to feel hard and bad feelings and I think they can love and be loved and, like we always said, that is all and everything.

I think back on a lot of our conversations about what would happen after you died. About what would become of Andy. About your fears that he would hide at the office or drink too much or yell at the kids. But he's not, Liz. He's reading C. S. Lewis and going to grief counseling and swimming three days a week. He's taking time off and learning to cook and taking it easy on the Manhattans. (He told me he can't afford to be hungover now that he's a mom.) Every Tuesday, he walks with Jen, the same loop you guys used to do. They talk about raising girls. She made him buy tampons and pads for every bathroom.

Recently, when he brought the kids up to our house for a visit, he told Edward that no dad knows his kids like a mom does. Edward pushed back. He said he had a great relationship with

Georgia and Claire. Andy said, "I know you do. I'm just saying you can't possibly know them *as well as* Kelly can." He said half the fights you guys had involved him accusing you of worrying too much and overthinking things. Now, he says, *I totally get it.*

He made a friend named Dennis whose wife died four years ago. They have coffee sometimes. I think it's a way for Andy to see a future. Dennis is dating; I think he's in love actually. I remind Andy how much you wanted him to find a new person, that you didn't want him to be alone. He knows that. He got kind of fixated on the idea of someone sleeping on your side of the bed and how that should never happen. But then, a few months went by and he walked in the bedroom and there was Gwen, in your spot, with your bedside light on, reading. That night *he* slept on your side of the bed. That worked for him. The new person, whenever that happens, whoever she is, can sleep on his old side.

He had his first passing crush on a woman— he said it made him feel teenagery—but he's not ready. I can't imagine the luck of the woman who will get to live with Andy Laats as he is now. He is twice the man for losing you, and in a way, she will be marrying both of you. He knows you gave Jen, Jessica, and me veto rights. He told me you left a letter behind for her.

He took off his wedding ring for an afternoon

but he hated being without it and had to put it back on. He figured out how to avoid uncomfortable conversations with strangers who want to know where his wife is. He says, "I'm a single parent," and that shuts them up. But to me, he explained that he is still married, that your relationship is still challenging him, driving him crazy, keeping him honest, and surfacing the better parts of him.

He cries a lot. His eyes get red and fill up and spill over and he keeps right on talking. He doesn't look away or apologize or clear his throat. It's so wonderful, the way he lets it happen. You are right there, on his lips, at the top of his throat, all the time.

Every night after the kids go to bed, he writes up the following day's plan on a whiteboard in the kitchen. He makes himself come up with a gimmick every day. Thirsty Thursday. Flip-Out Friday. Soggy Saturday. He lists the basic schedule plus any special events and reminders. There is usually a little drawing too. A soccer ball if Gwen has a game, a cupcake if there's a birthday that day.

He makes a lot of pancakes. Around the one-year mark, he found weevils in the flour. He didn't want to throw the bag out, because you bought it. You opened and closed that bag. You used that flour. He had to convince himself that you were not in the flour, that you are in the acts not the objects. So, he took the baking powder and some spices and the flour and dumped it all in the outside bins. He replaced everything, and when he wants you back, he and the kids bake.

His first birthday without you was a low. For his fiftieth, Jen picked him up in an Uber and they went out and got trashed. That weekend, he and the kids had a family barbecue. The foam-core blowup pictures of you from the memorial were still set up around the living room. He worried the house looked like the funeral was yesterday. He put some pictures away. It was a step.

Andy has a big list of the things he can't yet do but knows he must. Your closet is untouched. Your dresses, your shoes, your socks and old workout clothes. Your lotion and perfume and hair product. The last time I was there, I went back into your bathroom to touch something of yours. There was a hoodie on a hook, hung so casually it seemed like you must have worn it that morning. Andy knows he has to clean the closet out. We've talked about it. I told him I'd do it with him. He said thanks, but he was holding off on that for now. He did let me borrow an old pair of your sneakers, the ones with all the colors, to go on a walk with him and Jen. They were half a size too small. When we got back to your house, I wanted to take them home but he made me put them back.

Your ashes are still in a box. He's starting to think about that. He might take some to the beach, and then fly with the rest of them to Vermont, where you were supposed to be old together. He was a little mad that you didn't tell him exactly what to do with them. He didn't want to make a mistake. But then he decided that you wouldn't have wanted to tell him where to spread them, that you would want him to release them somewhere easy, somewhere he and the kids loved to go.

He fights regret. He didn't understand, in those last few weeks, how close you were to dying. You were always ahead of him; *the body knows.* He took Gwen to her soccer game the day you died. He has a hard time thinking about that, even though he was home in plenty of time. I told him that you died knowing you were loved, but he doesn't want to forgive himself yet.

We forgot something, you and me. In all the times we worried about whether Andy could be mother and father, whether he could endure the loneliness and frustration and thousand tiny failures, we forgot something essential about him: he's an A student, an enthusiastic, determined pupil. So he's learning how to be you. He is your apprentice. He reads and rereads your journals, he uses them like a map.

I should have understood this listening to him speak at the memorial. Oh, Liz, it was—I think about it all the time—it was transcendent. Must have been seven hundred people there. Every friend and teacher and old babysitter. Andy spent twenty minutes telling your love story. You would have wanted him to tighten it up but I told him it was okay to go through every beat. Every person there could have listened for hours. We wanted the long version. He talked about your eyes and your "supermodel cheekbones." He said he missed thinking with you and watching you make a decision. He loved your sense of right and wrong, your high standards, your single-minded focus on making a kind and relaxed home for Dru, Gwen, and Margo. He ended by trying to explain to us how people move onward from loss. It was the best thing I've ever heard about grief.

People ask how we're doing. Poets have tried for centuries to describe love, loss, death, and how these things transform the living. So I want to level-set people's expectations about what I'm about to say. It is beyond my abilities to describe how we're doing. There. Are your expectations sufficiently low? Good. I'll give it a try now.

Do you remember *Apollo 13*? As the son of an engineer who worked on the guidance system for that mission and other *Apollo* missions, I've paid some attention to the story. It goes something like this:

Apollo 13's mission was to explore a portion of the moon. Before the spacecraft reached the moon, there was an explosion on board that partially crippled it. An oxygen tank, I think. The damaged spaceship didn't have enough oxygen or power to complete its mission. So the mission to land on the moon was aborted and the astronauts worked feverishly with earth-based Mission Control to come up with another plan.

The damage was done. There wasn't enough power to simply turn around. There wasn't enough oxygen to take a safe, leisurely path back home, either. They needed a way to turn around and get back home quickly, using very little power in the process.

It was decided that the ship would use the gravitational power of the moon to propel it back to earth. If the ship could precisely enter a moon orbit, zip around the backside, and then exit the moon's orbit at exactly the right time, it could reset its trajectory, and, critically, conserve enough energy to be able to return safely to earth. All while keeping the structural integrity of the spacecraft intact and thereby protecting the astronauts.

Usually in *Apollo* missions there is one-hundred-percent constant connection between the spacecraft and Mission Control. In order for this plan to work, there would necessarily be silence as the ship shot around the back of the moon. The astronauts would disappear and, if everything worked out, they would reappear.

The speed of the ship heading into the partial lunar orbit was critical: too fast or too slow, and the power would be exhausted. The ship's direction was equally critical: just a fraction off the angle, and the exit trajectory would be wrong. The ship could crash if it came too close. Conversely, it would not catch the moon's gravitational pull if it was too far away, and without that, the ship would float into space. The crew and Mission Control faced catastrophe. And with this backdrop, they succeeded.

So, what's the metaphor?

The kids and I are the astronauts. We are in the ship, a little damaged, trying to figure out what to do next in the face of extreme uncertainty. Liz plays two roles. First, she's the moon. As the moon, she is providing us with the power to propel us back toward earth. We need her power; we don't have enough on our own. Her gravity acts both as tether and propulsion. We are sucked into her orbit for a brief while, gaining speed and reversing direction, only to expend our precious limited power to exit on our own path forward, her massive presence accelerating us homeward as required by God's laws of physics.

We cannot be with her; we cannot land and join her. We must accept that this mission must be aborted and the plans we made to explore, discover, challenge, and learn together cannot be carried out. This profound sense of loss is as devastating as the urgent feeling that focus on the future is necessary. The two feelings, loss and hope, hit us simultaneously.

You all are ground control. As ground control, you are taking the communication from us in the ship and the measurements from the instruments, grinding out the calculations, and guiding us back to safety. You can't be on the spacecraft with us. You can't possibly know how it feels to be alone in the vastness of space. But without your connection, we would be lost. We as astronauts feel the comfort of the connection, full faith that our path, while isolated in space's vast coldness, is being tracked at every second. That we are 200,000 miles from home but making progress each second. We work as a team, not frozen by catastrophe, but emboldened by it, inspired by it, sharpened by it. We make mistakes, we improvise solutions to unanticipated problems, we never lose hope.

I said Liz has two roles in my imperfect metaphor. The second role? She's JFK. As JFK, she got the entire Apollo program going. She set the whole thing up for success. She recruited only the best and brightest for ground control. She hired a captain (through a rigorous process, I might add) and staffed the ship with three strong, resourceful, hardworking, quick-thinking, graceful-under-pressure, handsome and beautiful astronauts. Then she trained us all. To pay attention. To say nice things to each other. To listen. To engage. To think for ourselves. To communicate. To *live* and *triumph* in the face of catastrophe. To wonder what we're doing here. To ask big questions of ourselves. To endure the struggle for answers. To set high standards for ourselves. To appreciate. To savor the moments of peace and progress. To grip each other strongly. To accept each other. To love.

(The Russians, by the way, are cancer.)

So that's how we're doing. Liz has put so many things in motion for me and Margo, Gwen, and Dru to be okay. As our "oxygen tanks" exploded, she course-corrected and put us on that perfect trajectory, with just the right amount of speed, to use her gravitational pull, and get turned around and headed back to home. We feel isolated, yes, but we are well trained and feel immense comfort in our connection with you all, a group hand-selected by Liz herself to "be in our lives." And, with your connection, we will ultimately make our way safely back to earth.

He and the kids are moving onward, not away from you but with you, the way I do with Greenie. You are everywhere they are. I love you through them.

Kelly

This Is It

When I got out of college, my goal was to become Interesting with a capital *I*. I fancied Mary Oliver poems, the word *intrepid,* and my motto, *Things happen when you leave the house,* the house being an easy signifier for everything familiar. My path was adventure. I saved for two years, living on my cousin's couch to save on rent. Eventually, I filled a fanny pack with all the money I had ($3,800 in traveler's checks), a Lonely Planet guide, the phone number of a guy my dad used to know, and some antibiotics my mom made me bring. Tracy Tuttle by my side, I set off to see the world.

After a couple of months living large in Hong Kong, Thailand, and Melbourne, we found ourselves on a 12-hour bus ride to Sydney, counting our money, deciding we needed jobs. We became (of all things) nannies: Tracy for a family of six, me for two kids whose mother had recently died. Something changed. Not immediately, but I left that house less smitten with world travelers and their ripping yarns and more awed by people who had thrown themselves into what I was starting to see was, for me, the one gig that mattered: parenthood.

Heading into my thirties, the life I have now—

healthy kids and a sensible man to raise them with—was exactly the life I wanted. I knew that the coolest thing about the coolest people I knew was that they had made real families, families with inside jokes and nicknames and weird pets they'd be talking about into their eighties.

That's the shore I set out for. But bobbing around out there in my double-breasted Dress Barn power suit, I was drowning. Blame it on the freshman fifteen I never lost or the Merit Ultra Lights I couldn't give up or my sailor mouth, but it took a long fucking time to find Mr. Right and get a family going.

Now, only sixteen years into motherhood, I already want to go back . . . to the time when tattoos were temporary and bedroom doors were open, when I knew precisely where my kids were and what they were doing, when I could pick up my girls without spraining my lumbar.

Don't get me wrong; I want the now, too. When I am traveling and call home, it is so good to hear their voices, I can't imagine being angry with any of them ever again. Same when they're sleeping or when I see people hug on the curb at the airport or during the days around a memorial service. The week I spent writing Liz's eulogy, I swore I would never again hurry Edward along as he ranted about another bullshit technical foul on Draymond Green and I would definitely stop giving the finger to my daughters' backs as they stormed away.

But cycling between the kitchen, the desk, and the carpool? It can be hard to revel in the domestic litter of moldy towels and muddy cleats, much less the cacophony of clashing siblings or worse: the near silence of click-clicking thumbs on smartphones, Rihanna whining from a bedroom radio left on. And what's the sound of eyes rolling, of marital friction or the mind bending around itself trying to decide when to step in, when to let them fail or fight or go to that kid's house you have a bad feeling about?

It's a lonely business, and then sometimes strangely claustrophobic, but this is it. This is what I wanted and what Liz was pulled away from, against her every fiber. This abstract performance art called *Family Life* is our one run at the ultimate improv. Our chance to be great for someone, to give another person enough of what they need to be happy. Ours to overlook or lose track of or bemoan, ours to recommit to, to apologize for, to try again for. Ours to watch disappear into their next self—toddler to tyke, tween to teen—ours to drop off somewhere and miss forever.

It's happening right now, whether we attend to it or not.

Like after preparing a nutritious meal that no one really liked and a lot of blame-gaming over who forgot to take out the compost, your peevish, greasy "young adult" tramps off to take the shower she should have taken two days ago and the evening is shot to shit and not one minute of it looked like the thing you prayed for so long ago, but then you hear something.

You head up the stairs, hover outside the bathroom door.

"All the single ladies, all the single ladies . . ."

The kid is singing in the shower. Your profoundly ordinary kid is singing in the shower and you get to be here to hear it.

AUTHOR'S NOTE

I recently drove from Oakland to Los Angeles with the girls and Edward, and on the way home, we argued about who ordered the sausage pizza *the night before*. Everyone remembered the ordering differently and we were each sure, absolutely, that our memory was accurate and complete.

In this book, I tell many stories, some of which involve others: my husband and mom, my brothers and daughters, my best friend from high school, my old boss at Villanova Pizza. It's anyone's guess how they would tell the same stories.

All I can promise is that I haven't messed with the truth as I know it and, in many cases, I pulled directly from old journals (which are still, alas, only my version of events, recorded in a timely manner). Reality always comes dressed in a point of view, try as we might to lay it bare.

I NEED HELP

You would be horrified if you read any one of the first half-dozen drafts of this book. So, in a way, we can all thank Ariel Trost, Sarah Handelsman, Phoebe Lichty, and Susan George, who opened emails from me called I Need Help. These women, who have jobs and passion projects and families who need them, read multiple drafts and asked hard, important questions; Jen de la Fuente who was mercifully blunt (prefacing her feedback with "I really like you and I don't want to destroy our friendship but . . ."); Melissa Williams who told me she wanted to laugh more and then later that same night sent a loving follow-up saying, "About the funny thing: I know it's been a hard few years so don't feel like you owe us laughter"); Andy Sheehan who has consistently flooded me with courage since sixth grade and who said, "You know how special this is, don't you?"; and the writers Susannah Meadows and Kimberly Ford Chisholm, who went page by page with me, redlining, challenging, validating.

After a year, I shared the pages with a two-person power team of Suzanne Gluck at William Morris Endeavor and Andy Ward at Random House. Suzanne who says, "Congratulations, we have a book here!" at the first sign that something coherent is coming together. Suzanne who has a huge career and is ten times smarter than I am and so, when she says "I am really, *really* happy to be in the boat on this," I feel like I might survive publication. Suzanne who finagles, in the nicest way, another round of cover designs. You are best in class, Gluck. Everyone says so and it's true. Then there's Andy. Andy who has way better things to do than try to teach me how to "be more observant" and "go deeper" and "when in doubt, stick with storytelling." Andy who "hates alliteration" and tells me I can "be funnier than this, yo" and slashed half of my favorite, *maybe* overwrought, lines saying, "I blow shit up, that's what I do." Andy who takes the work seriously but never deadly so. Andy who never insults me with feedback sandwiches. Andy who said, finally, twenty-one months into it, "I love it. You rule."

There is also a brave and good woman at Random House named Sharon Propson who partners with me after the manuscript goes to the printers and it's time to connect with readers. SP, thanks for having my back. We were *definitely* meant to work together.

Lastly, my career began with the bright light of goodness and smarts that is Andy Barzvi of Empire Literary. We had a great run together and I was lucky to meet her when I did.

THANK YOU

To my mom, a private woman whose feedback on my writing often focuses on grammar and spelling and who might prefer that my calling not involve sharing her personal business, but who is, ultimately, so thoroughly maternal that she stops by bookstores to move copies of my books to high-traffic areas like the front table or next to the Altoids at the register. Ma, one way or another, it all goes back to you.

To my brothers, Booker and George, who didn't choose to have a sister who writes books and flies from city to city telling family stories. Sometimes it's kind of neat but at other times, I can imagine, it's a bit much. Thank you for going with the flow and even sometimes showing up for readings. I can't tell you what a big deal it is to me to see you there. As your little sister, the pathetic truth is: my need to impress you never ends.

To my girl Tracy Tuttle, whose married name is McGowan; my two wise men, Will Kabat-Zinn and Rabbi Michael Lezak; the lovely and fearless Harriet Haydemann.

To Andy Laats, whom I can't talk about without gushing. I know it's harder than it looks. I know you get so tired. But honestly, you are exceptional. Thank you for holding the space where your one and only Liz used to be.

To my girls, Georgia and Claire, the biggest things that ever happened to me, the central force of my life. Let me just say this: nobody will ever be as interesting or beautiful to me as you are. I joke that "the best moment of the day" is taking off my bra, but of course it's seeing you come down in the morning.

And to Edward Lichty, whom I like to call Eddy (but you may not), for letting me be a real bitch sometimes and flat-out dumb other times and holding my hand anyway. The fact that you take me seriously—and like me enough to make a whole long life together—is *the ground* I stand on.

ABOUT THE AUTHOR

Kelly Corrigan has been called "the voice of her generation" by *O: The Oprah Magazine* and "the poet laureate of the ordinary" by *HuffPost*. She is the author of the *New York Times* bestsellers *The Middle Place*, *Lift*, and *Glitter and Glue.* She is also the creative director of The Nantucket Project and host of their conversation series about what matters most. With a few friends, she created Notes & Words, an annual benefit concert featuring writers and musicians on stage together that has raised $8 million for the UCSF Benioff Children's Hospital. She lives near Oakland, California, with her husband, Edward Lichty, and her teenage daughters, Georgia and Claire.

kellycorrigan.com
Facebook.com/kellycorriganauthor
Twitter: @corrigankelly
Instagram: @kellycorrigan
YouTube.com/kellycorriganvideo
Look online for Kelly Corrigan's
KQED podcast Exactly.

Center Point Large Print
600 Brooks Road / PO Box 1
Thorndike, ME 04986-0001 USA

(207) 568-3717

US & Canada:
1 800 929-9108
www.centerpointlargeprint.com